박 시 균

Business English Conversation
비즈니스 영어회화

도서출판
진영사

비즈니스영어회화

Business English Conversation

박시균

2008년 10월 25일 초판 인쇄
2017년 09월 10일 초판4쇄 발행

발행인 ‖ 박진영
발행처 ‖ 도서출판 진영사
인천광역시 부평구 부평동 134-16 태승빌딩 4층
tel. 032-505-4207
fax. 032-505-4206
e-mail. 0183734207@hanmail.net

ISBN 978-89-93076-54-7 03740

preface 머리말

대학에서 교육을 하면서 어려움을 겪었던 부분이 바로 학생들의 회화 실력이 떨어진다는 것이었다. 특히 회사에서 가장 요긴하게 쓰일 전화대화법이나 예약, 물건 구입 등에서 많은 어려움을 겪고 있었다. 또한 일선 회사들의 대학을 졸업한 신입사원들에 대한 불만도 영어 측정 시험의 점수는 좋지만 실무 회화에서 많은 문제점을 안고 있다는 것이었다.

본서는 이런 학생들의 어려움과 일선 회사의 불만들을 한데 모아 그 부분을 집중적으로 다루어 학생들이 회화 능력의 향상을 기하여 장차 실무에 뛰어 들어서도 영어회화 능력을 인정받을 수 있도록 구성되었다.

본서는 2부로 나뉘어져 있는데 1부는 기본 영어회화 부분이다. 이 부분을 통해서 학생들은 전화받기, 예약, 안내에 이르기까지 외국인과 전화상으로 혹은 실제로 만났을 때 영어로 대화하는 법을 배우고 학생들 본인이 외국에 가거나 혹은 외국인을 접대할 때 어떻게 대화를 이끌어 나갈 것인가에 대해서도 배우게 된다.

2부에서는 장차 학생들이 회사에 들어가서 접하게 될 설명과 협상, 조건과 주문, 신용장과 선적, 클레임과 손해배상, 해외 출장 등 분야의 좀 더 전문화된 회화를 배우게 된다. 이 2부의 내용을 통해 학생들은 장차 산업 현장에서 부딪히게 될 다양한 회화 능력을 배양함으로써 회사에 들어가서도 바로 실무에 투입되어 그들의 능력을 사용할 수 있을 것이다.

영어는 이해과목이 아니라 암기과목이다. 일단은 회화의 내용을 이해하는 것이 우선이겠지만 문형을 머리 속에 넣지 않는다면 아무 소용이 없다. 아무쪼록 본서를 공부하면서 학생들이 많은 문형을 암기, 체득하여 실무에서도 바로 사용할 수 있게 되기를 바라마지 않는다.

저 자

contents

차 례

PART 1 기본영어회화편

PART 2 무역영어회화편

APPENDICES

PART 1

기본영어회화편

PART 1

1. 전화

1-1 전화 걸고 받기

A. Dialogue

- Listen to the teacher.
- Repeat after the teacher.
- Practice by yourself.
- Memorize the dialogue.

1. A: May I speak with Mr. Parker?
   B: This is he.
   A: Hi, Mr. Parker. This is Miss Lee returning your call.
   B: Oh, yes, Miss Lee. I've been expecting your call.

2. A: STAR Company. May I help you?
   B: Yes, May I speak to Mr. Disney, please?
   A: I'm sorry, but he just stepped out.
   B: When do you expect him back?
   A: I'm not sure. Care to leave your name and phone number?
   B: I'm on the move and this is a pay phone. Just tell him Jack Smith called, please.
   A: I sure will.

Business English Conversation

B. Practice

- Read through the dialogue in Korean.
- Repeat the dialogue in English.

1. A: 파커씨와 통화 좀 할 수 있을까요?
   B: 제가 파컨데요.
   A: 안녕하세요. 파커씨. 저는 미스리예요. 전화를 해달라고 하셨다기에 전화 드리는 겁니다.
   B: 아, 네. 미스리. 전화 기다리고 있었습니다.

2. A: Star 회사입니다. 뭘 도와드릴까요?
   B: 네, 디즈니씨와 통화할 수 있을까요?
   A: 죄송합니다만 방금 나가셨는데요.
   B: 언제 들어오실까요?
   A: 잘 모르겠습니다. 성함과 전화번호를 남겨주시겠습니까?
   B: 저는 지금 이동 중이고 이건 공중전화입니다. 잭 스미스가 전화했다고만 전해 주세요.
   A: 그렇게 하겠습니다.

3. A: May I speak to Mr. Jackson?
B: Speaking.
A: Hi, Mr. Jackson. My name is Dong-Il Kim.
Mr. Ingram referred me to you about opening an L/C.
B: Oh, yes, Mr. Kim. Can we get together this afternoon?
A: Fine with me.
B: When is the most convenient time for you?
A: Anytime after two will be fine.

4. A: Sam-Jin Trading Company.
B: Could you connect me with Mr. Lee Sung-Gyoo's office, please?
A: He is on the phone, now. Could you hold?
B: No, I think I'll call back tomorrow.
A: Okay, I'll tell him you will call again tomorrow.
B: Thank you.

5. A: Jim Baker? He no longer works here.
B: Is that right? When did he quit?
A: He quit about two months ago.
B: Then, can I speak to Mr. Ted Turner?
A: I'm sorry. There is no one here by that name.

3. A: 잭슨씨와 통화할 수 있을까요?
B: 전데요.
A: 안녕하십니까, 잭슨씨. 제 이름은 김동일입니다.
신용장 개설에 관해서 인그램씨가 당신에게 전화를 해보라고 해서 전화를 드리는 겁니다.
B: 아, 그러시군요, 김선생님. 오늘 오후에 함께 만날 수 있을까요?
A: 저는 괜찮아요.
B: 가장 편리한 시간이 언제시죠?
A: 2시 이후에는 아무 때나 좋습니다.

4. A: 삼진 무역 회사입니다.
B: 이성규씨 사무실로 연결시켜 주시겠습니까?
A: 지금 통화 중 이신데요. 기다리시겠습니까?
B: 아니오. 내일 다시 걸어야 겠어요.
A: 알겠습니다. 내일 다시 전화하실 거라고 전해 드리겠습니다.
B: 고맙습니다.

5. A: 짐 베이커씨요? 그 분은 여기서 더 이상 일하시지 않는데요.
B: 그렇습니까? 언제 그만 두셨지요?
A: 두 달전 쯤이요.
B: 그러면 테드 터너씨와 통화할 수 있을까요?
A: 죄송한데요. 그런 이름을 가진 분은 여기에 없는데요.

C. Important Points

1. • This is Miss Lee returning your call.
   전화를 해달라고 하셨다기에 전화드리는 겁니다.
   • I've been expecting your call.
   전화 기다리고 있었습니다.

2. • care to-: -하고 싶어하다 = would you care to-?
   • pay phone: 공중전화
   • phone booth: 공중전화 박스
   • on the move: 이동 중에

3. • L/C: letter of credit 신용장
   • get together 모이다, 화합하다.

4. • He is on the phone, now.: 지금 전화중이신데요.
   • Could you hold?: 기다리시겠습니까?

5. • He no longer works here.
   그 분은 여기서 더 이상 일하시지 않는데요.
   • There is no one here by that name.
   그런 이름을 가진 분은 여기에 없는데요.

D. Filling in the Blanks

1. A: STAR Company. May I help you?
   B: Yes, ________________ Mr. Disney, please?
   A: I'm sorry, but he just ________________.
   B: When do you expect him back?
   A: I'm not sure. Care to leave your name and phone number?
   B: I'm ____________ and this is a pay phone. Just tell him Jack Smith called, please.
   A: I sure will.

2. A: _______________ Mr. Jackson?
   B: Speaking.
   A: Hi, Mr. Jackson. My name is Dong-Il Kim.
   Mr. Ingram referred me to you about opening an L/C.
   B: Oh, yes, Mr. Kim. Can we ____________ this afternoon?
   A: Fine with me.
   B: When is the most convenient time for you?
   A: Anytime __________ will be fine.

3. A: Sam-Jin Trading Company.
   B: Could you connect me with Mr. Lee Sung-Gyoo's office, please?
   A: He is _____________, now. Could you hold?
   B: No, I think _______________ tomorrow.
   A: Okay, I'll tell him you will call again tomorrow.
   B: Thank you.

E. Dictation

1. ______________________________

2. ______________________________

3. ______________________________

4. ______________________________

5. ______________________________

6. ______________________________

7. ______________________________

8. ______________________________

9. ______________________________

10. ______________________________

11. ______________________________

12. ______________________________

13. ______________________________

14. ______________________________

15. ______________________________

E. Dictation 2

1. ______________________________

2. ______________________________

3. ______________________________

4. ______________________________

5. ______________________________

6. ______________________________

7. ______________________________

8. ______________________________

9. ______________________________

10. ______________________________

11. ______________________________

12. ______________________________

13. ______________________________

14. ______________________________

15. ______________________________

1-2 국제 전화 걸고 받기

A. Dialogue

- Listen to the teacher.
- Repeat after the teacher.
- Practice by yourself.
- Memorize the dialogue.

1. A: Operator! Can I make a collect call to Seoul Korea?

   B: Yes, you can. What's the name of the party and the number, please?

   ……

   Hello, I have a collect call for Mr. Young-Ho Kim from Tim Woods in L.A., will you accept the charges?

   C: Yes, I will.

   B: O.K. Go ahead.

2. A: This is the overseas operator. May I help you?

   B: I'd like to place a station to station call to Seoul, Korea. The area code is 2 and the number in Seoul is 213-4325.

   A: May I have your telephone number?

   B: It is 61-7-357-7763.

   A: May I have your name?

   B: This is Mr. Chun-Soo Lee.

   A: Thank you. Will you hang up and wait, please?

   B: Okay. Thank you.

B. Practice

- Read through the dialogue in Korean.
- Repeat the dialogue in English.

1. A: 교환원이시죠! 한국 서울로 수신자 부담 전화를 할 수 있을까요?
   B: 물론이죠. 전화 받을 분의 성함과 전화번호는 무엇이지요?
   ……
   여보세요, L.A.의 팀 우즈씨로부터 김영호씨에게 수신자 부담 전화가 신 청되어있는데요.
   전화 요금을 물고 전화를 받으시겠습니까?
   C: 그렇게 하겠습니다.
   B: 좋습니다. 통화하세요.

2. A: 국제 전화 교환원입니다. 뭘 도와드릴까요?
   B: 한국의 서울로 번호 통화를 하고 싶습니다. 지역 번호는 2이고 번호는 213-4325입니다.
   A: 전화 거신 분의 전화번호를 알 수 있을까요?
   B: 예 61-7-357-7763입니다.
   A: 성함은 어떻게 되시죠?
   B: 전 이천수입니다.
   A: 고맙습니다. 전활 끊고 잠시 기다려 주시겠어요?
   B: 알겠습니다. 감사합니다.

3. A: Overseas operator. May I help you?

B: Yes, I'd like to place an overseas person to person call to Korea.

A: What city and number are you calling, Sir?

B: Seoul. The area code is 2 and the number is 335-2687.

A: Who would you like to talk to?

B: Manager Mr. Shin Sun.

A: Could you spell Shin Sun for me?

B: Ceratinly, it's spelled S-H-I-N and S-U-N.

A: Okay, S-H-I-N and S-U-N. Thank you. You are calling Mr. Shin at 82-2-335-2687. Is that right?

B: Yes, that's right.

A: Can I ask your number?

B: My number is 61-2-312-3531.

A: Thank you. We'll call you back in a few minutes.

4. A: Operator. May I help you?

B: Yes, I'd like to make an international call to Korea.

A: You can dial that direct.

B: How do I do that?

A: First, dial 01 for an international call.

B: Yes.

A: Then dial the country code. That's 82 for Korea.

B: A-ha.

A: Then the area code and phone number.

B: So, dial 01-82-031-328-7732?

A: Actually, no. You have to use the two digit area code. You shouldn't dial the zero at the area code.

B: I see. Is it the same for mobile phones and beepers?

A: Yes, it is.

B: I think I've got it. Thank you very much.

A: Thank you.

3. A: 국제 전화 교환원입니다. 뭘 좀 도와드릴까요?
B: 네. 한국으로 대화자 지명통화를 하려고 합니다.
A: 전화하시려는 도시와 전화번호가 무엇이죠?
B: 서울이고요. 지역번호는 2번, 번호는 335-2687입니다.
A: 누구와 통화하기를 원하십니까?
B: 신선 부장입니다.
A: 신선씨의 철자를 알려주시겠습니까?
B: 물론이죠. S-H-I-N 그리고 S-U-N입니다.
A: 알겠습니다. S-H-I-N 그리고 S-U-N. 고맙습니다. 82-2-335-2687번의 신선씨에게 통화하시려고 하는 거죠, 그렇죠?
B: 네, 맞습니다.
A: 선생님의 번호는 몇 번이죠?
B: 제 번호는 61-2-312-3531입니다.
A: 고맙습니다. 몇 분 있다 다시 전화드리겠습니다.

4. A: 교환원입니다. 뭘 좀 도와드릴까요?
B: 예. 한국으로 국제 전화를 하려고 합니다.
A: 직접 거실 수 있습니다.
B: 어떻게 하지요?
A: 우선 국제 전화를 걸기 위해서 01번을 누르세요.
B: 네.
A: 그리고는 국가 번호를 누르세요. 한국은 82번입니다.
B: 아. 그렇군요.
A: 그리고는 지역 번호와 전화번호를 누르면 됩니다.
B: 그렇다면 01-82-031-328-7732를 누르면 됩니까?
A: 아니오. 지역 번호는 두 자리 코드를 사용해야 합니다. 지역 번호에서 코드에는 0을 눌러서는 안 됩니다.
B: 알겠습니다. 휴대전화와 삐삐도 마찬가지입니까?
A: 네, 그렇습니다.
B: 알 것 같군요. 대단히 감사합니다.
A: 고맙습니다.

5. A: Operator. How may I help you?

B: I'd like to place a station to station call to Korea.
Charge the call to my credit card please.

A: Your credit card number, please.

B: It's 2234-8732-5712.

A: What number are you calling?

B: 82-2-972-3781.

A: All right. May I have your number?

B: This is 61-2-554-3278.

A: Thank you. I'll call you back in 10 minutes time. Will you hang up and wait, please?

5. A: 교환원입니다. 무얼 도와드릴까요?
B: 한국으로 번호 통화를 하고 싶은데요.
요금은 제 신용카드로 계산해 주세요.
A: 신용카드 번호를 알려 주세요.
B: 그것은 2234-8732-5712입니다.
A: 몇 번에 거시려고 하십니까?
B: 82-2-972-3781입니다.
A: 알겠습니다. 선생님의 번호를 알려 주시겠어요?
B: 제 번호는 61-2-554-3278입니다.
A: 고맙습니다. 10분 후에 전화 다시 드리겠습니다. 전화를 끊고 기다리시겠습니까?

C. Important Points

1. - collect call = reverse charge call: 수신자 부담 전화
   - the party: (전화 받은) 상대방, 당사자

2. - a station to station call: 번호를 통한 통화
   - Will you hang up and wait, please?
     전활 끊고 잠시 기다려 주시겠어요?

3. - a person to person call: 대화자 지명통화
   - I'd like to place an overseas person to person call to Korea.
     한국으로 대화자 지명통화를 하려고 합니다.

4. - mobile phone: 휴대폰 (=cellular phone, cell phone)
   - beeper: 삐삐

5. - Charge the call to my credit card please.
     요금은 제 신용카드로 계산해 주세요.
   - What number are you calling?: 몇 번에 거시려고 하십니까?

D. Filling in the Blanks

1. A: This is the overseas operator. May I help you?

   B: I'd like to ______________________ to Seoul, Korea.

   The area code is 2 and the number in Seoul is 213-4325.

   A: May I have ______________________?

   B: It is 61-7-357-7763.

   A: May I have your name?

   B: This is Mr. Chun-Soo Lee.

2. A: ______________________ are you calling, Sir?

   B: Seoul. The area code is 2 and the number is 335-2687.

   A: Who would you like to talk to?

   B: Manager Mr. Shin Sun.

   A: ____________________ Shin Sun for me?

   B: Certainly, it's spelled S-H-I-N and S-U-N.

   A: Okay, S-H-I-N and S-U-N. Thank you. _____________ Mr. Shin at 82-2-335-2687. Is that right?

   B: Yes, that's right.

3. A: Operator. ______________________?

   B: I'd like to place a station to station call to Korea.

   Charge the call __________________ please.

   A: Your credit card number, please.

   B: It's 2234-________-5712.

   A: What number are you calling?

   B: 82-2-972-3781.

   A: All right. May I have your number?

   B: This is 61-2-554-3278.

E. Dictation

1. ______

2. ______

3. ______

4. ______

5. ______

6. ______

7. ______

8. ______

9. ______

10. ______

11. ______

12. ______

13. ______

14. ______

15. ______

E. Dictation 2

1. ______________________________

2. ______________________________

3. ______________________________

4. ______________________________

5. ______________________________

6. ______________________________

7. ______________________________

8. ______________________________

9. ______________________________

10. ______________________________

11. ______________________________

12. ______________________________

13. ______________________________

14. ______________________________

15. ______________________________

1-3 전화메시지 및 잘못 걸린 전화

A. Dialogue

- Listen to the teacher.
- Repeat after the teacher.
- Practice by yourself.
- Memorize the dialogue.

1. A: May I speak to Mrs. Park?

B: Hold on a second, please.

I'm sorry. She's not in now.

A: When will she return?

B: I'm not sure. Is it an urgent matter?

A: No, I'll call her back later.

B: Who is this, please?

A: This is Ron Zimmer.

………………………………

A: Hello. This is Ron Zimmer again.

Is Mrs Park there?

B: I'm sorry, she hasn't come home yet.

May I take a message?

A: Tell her I called, please. Thank you. Goodbye.

B. Practice

- Read through the dialogue in Korean.
- Repeat the dialogue in English.

1. A: 박여사님 좀 바꿔주십시오.
B: 잠시만 기다려 주세요.
죄송합니다. 그 분은 지금 여기에 안 계십니다.
A: 언제 돌아오실까요?
B: 확실히 모르겠습니다. 급한 일이세요?
A: 아니오, 나중에 다시 전화 걸겠습니다.
B: 전화 거신 분은 누구시죠?
A: 저는 론 짐머입니다.
……………(시간이 흐른 후)…………………
A: 여보세요. 아까 전화한 론 짐머입니다.
박여사님 계십니까?
B: 죄송하지만 그 분은 아직 돌아오지 않았습니다.
전하실 말씀이 있습니까?
A: 제가 전화했다고 전해주십시오. 감사합니다. 안녕히 계십시오.

2. A: Hello. This is Paul. Is Sue there?
B: There is no one here by that name.
A: Is this 378-5762?
B: You have the right number but the wrong party.
A: Could you give me your home address, please?
B: I live at 103, Church St.
A: Have you lived there long?
B: No, we just moved here recently.
A: Oh, unbelievable!
B: I'm sorry to hear that.
A: It's all right. Sorry to have bothered you.

3. A: Were there any messages left for me?
B: Let me check.
Oh, you got a call from Mr. Baker. He wants you to call him back.
A: What did he call about?
B: He said something about a party you were invited to.
A: What's the number? Let me call him right away.
B: It's 278-3957.

4. A: May I speak to Mr. Jung please?
B: I'm sorry. He's out on business.
A: May I ask when he's coming back?
B: He won't be back in the office today., I'm afraid. May I take a message?
A: Yes, will you tell him to call me first thing tomorrow morning?
B: Certainly, I will. Thank you for calling.

2. A: 여보세요. 저는 폴인데요. 수 있습니까?

B: 그런 사람은 여기에 없습니다.

A: 거기가 378-5762번입니까?

B: 번호는 맞는데 사람이 틀립니다.

A: 당신의 주소를 가르쳐 주시겠어요?

B: 저는 교회거리 103번지에 살고 있습니다.

A: 당신은 그 곳에 산지 오래됐습니까?

B: 아니오, 우리는 최근에 여기에 이사 왔습니다.

A: 오, 믿을 수 없어!

B: 그거 참 안됐군요.

A: 괜찮습니다. 폐를 끼쳐서 죄송합니다.

3. A: 누구한테서 연락 온 것 없었어요?

B: 제가 확인해 보겠습니다. 아, 베이커씨에게서 왔었어요. 전화 좀 걸어 달라고 하던데요.

A: 전화의 용건은 뭐던가요?

B: 초대받으신 파티에 관한 일이라고 하셨어요.

A: 전화번호가 어떻게 되지요? 당장 전화해봐야 겠어요.

B: 278-3957이에요.

4. A: 정 선생님 좀 바꿔주시겠어요?

B: 죄송합니다. 업무관계로 외출중인데요.

A: 언제쯤 돌아오실까요?

B: 오늘은 회사로 안 돌아오실 것 같은데요. 죄송하지만 전할 말씀이라도 있으십니까?

A: 네, 내일 아침 제일 우선적으로 제게 전화 좀 해 달라고 전해주시겠습니까?

B: 물론이죠, 그렇게 전해 드리죠. 전화해 주셔서 감사합니다.

5. A: Hello, Export Department. May I help you?

B: Mr. Yong-Su Park, please.

A: May I ask what this is in regard to, sir?

B: I'm Mr. Harris from ABC Co.
It's about the new leather jacket order.

A: Mr. Park is in a meeting right now.
Could you call back in about an hour?

B: Yes, certainly.

5. A: 여보세요. 수출부입니다. 무얼 도와드릴까요?

B: 박용수선생님 좀 부탁합니다.

A: 무슨 일이신지 여쭤봐도 될까요?

B: 저는 미국의 ABC사의 해리스라고 합니다.
새 가죽 자켓 주문에 관한 용 건인데요.

A: 박선생님은 지금 회의중이신데, 한 시간 쯤 후에 다시 전화 해 주시겠습니까?

B: 네, 그렇게 하죠.

C. Important Points

1. - wonder: ~이 아닐까 생각하다
   - I wonder when she will come.: 언제쯤 오실 지 모르겠습니다.

2. 〈전화를 잘못 걸었을 때의 사과의 표현들〉
   - Sorry to trouble you. 폐를 끼쳐서 죄송합니다.
   - I'm sorry I must have the wrong number.
     전화를 잘못 걸어서 죄송합니다.
   - I'm sorry. I must have dialed the wrong number.
     죄송합니다. 제가 잘못 걸었나 봅니다.
   - I'm terribly sorry. 정말 죄송합니다.
   - I apologize. 죄송합니다.

3. - Were there any calls while I was out?
     나 없는 사이에 연락 온 데 없었어요?
   - You got a call from Mr. Lee. He wants you to call him back.
     이선생님한테서 전화가 왔었는데 전화 좀 걸어달라던데요.
   - You got a call. = You had a call. = You received a call.
   - You received a call from Mr. Lee. He said he would appreciate it if you would return his call as soon as you came in. (formal한 표현)
     김선생님한테서 전화가 왔었는데 들어오시는 대로 전화 좀 부탁한다고 하던데요.
   - Ring Mr. Lee back. (아주 informal한 표현) 이선생님한테 전화 걸어줘.
   - Call Mr. Kim. He buzzed while you were out. (아주 informal한 표현)
     김선생님한테 전화해봐. 너 없을 때 전화왔었어.

4.
- He's not in at the moment. 지금 안계십니다.
- He's gone for the day. 오늘은 이만 퇴근하셨습니다.
- May I leave a message? 메모 좀 해주시겠습니까?
- Would you take a message? 전갈 좀 받아주시겠습니까?
- Can I take a message? 전갈을 받아드릴까요?
- Would you leave a message? 전할 말씀 있으세요?
- Would you care to leave a message? 뭐라고 전해드릴까요?

5. 〈용건을 묻는 표현〉
- May I ask what this is in regard to, sir?
  어떤 용건인지 여쭈어봐도 될 까요?
- What are you calling about? 어떤 일로 전화를 하셨습니까?
- What is your call regarding? 어떤 일에 관한 것이지요?
- Regarding what, sir? 어떤 일이지요?

D. Filling in the Blanks

1. A: May I speak to Mrs. Park?
   B: ____________________, please.
   I'm sorry. She's not in now.
   A: ____________________?
   B: I'm not sure. Is it an urgent matter?
   A: No, I'll ____________________.
   B: Who is this, please?
   A: This is Ron Zimmer.

2. A: Were there any messages left for me?
   B: ____________________.
   Oh, you got a call from Mr. Baker. ____________________ him back.
   A: What did he call about?
   B: He said something about a party you were invited to.
   A: What's the number? ____________________.
   B: It's 278-3957.

3. A: Hello, Export Department. May I help you?
   B: Mr. Yong-Su Park, please.
   A: May I ask what this is ______________, sir?
   B: I'm Mr. Harris from ABC Co. It's about the new leather jacket order.
   A: Mr. Park ______________ right now. Could you call back in about an hour?
   B: Yes, certainly.

E. Dictation

1. ____________________

2. ____________________

3. ____________________

4. ____________________

5. ____________________

6. ____________________

7. ____________________

8. ____________________

9. ____________________

10. ____________________

11. ____________________

12. ____________________

13. ____________________

14. ____________________

15. ____________________

1-4 전화 약속

A. Dialogue

- Listen to the teacher.
- Repeat after the teacher.
- Practice by yourself.
- Memorize the dialogue.

1. A: Hello. May I speak to Jane Spencer?
C: Who is this?
A: This is Tom Jones.
C: Wait a minute.
B: Hello.
A: Hi, Jane. You're just the person I wanted to see.
B: What's on your mind?
A: Well, I'd like to discuss a little business with you. I was going to call and see when you're free.
B: How about dropping into my office tomorrow morning? Say ten.
A: All right. Well, I'll see you tomorrow. Thank you very much.
B: That's all right. I'll be waiting for you.
A: Yes. So long.
B: So long.

2. A: Hello. A.B.C. Shipping Co.
B: Yes. This is Mr. Shim Ki-Hyun. Is Mr. Smith available this afternoon?
A: Let me check, please. Oh, I see Mr. Smith has 20 minutes at 2:30, 30 minutes at 4:00.
B: Could I come by at 2:30?
A: Surely. I'll put you down for that time.
B: Thank you.

B. Practice

- Read through the dialogue in Korean.
- Repeat the dialogue in English.

1. A: 여보세요. 제인 스펜서씨 좀 바꿔 주십시오.
C: 누구세요?
A: 저는 톰 존스입니다.
C: 잠깐만 기다리십시오.
B: 여보세요.
A: 안녕하세요, 제인. 당신을 좀 만나고 싶은데요.
B: 무슨 일인데요?
A: 당신과 사업에 대해 좀 의논하고 싶어서요. 당신이 언제 시간이 나는지 알고 싶어 전화 드렸습니다.
B: 내일 아침 우리 사무실에 들르시는 게 어때요? 한 10시 쯤 에요.
A: 좋아요. 그럼, 내일 뵙겠습니다. 정말 고맙습니다.
B: 천만에요. 당신을 기다리고 있겠습니다.
A: 예. 안녕히 계세요.
B: 안녕히 계세요.

2. A: 여보세요. ABC 선박회사입니다.
B: 네, 전 심기현이라고 하는데요. 스미스씨께서 오늘 오후에 시간이 있으신지요?
A: 확인 좀 해볼께요. 아, 김선생님께선 2시 30분에 20분, 4시에 30분 정도 시간이 있으십니다.
B: 2시 30분에 잠시 들러도 되겠습니까?
A: 네, 그러세요. 그 시간에 선생님이 오시는 것으로 적어 놓겠습니다.
B: 감사합니다.

3. A: Hello. May I speak to Young-Soo?
B: Speaking. Who is calling?
A: This is Hee-Young.
B: What can I do for you, Hee-Young?
A: Well, I'd like to see you one of these days. I'm leaving Korea for Canada to study abroad soon.
B: Oh, are you? I didn't know that.
A: Well, it was sort of a sudden decision.
B: How long will you be gone?
A: About three years.
B: That long? Well, I'll be happy to meet you any time after six o'clock.
A: Excellent. How about tomorrow?
B: That will be fine. Where shall we meet?
A: How about the Green Park at seven?
B: Suits me fine.
A: All right. See you tomorrow then!
B: Good-bye.

4. A: Hello. Tom Baker's residence.
B: Hi! Mr. Baker. This is Park Soo-Il. I'm having a little get-together over at my place tonight at about six. Will you be able to join us?
A: Who's going to be there?
B: Oh, just some of the co-workers from the office.
A: Well, I'll tell you. I'll be pretty tied up until around 6:30 or so.
B: Why not make it at seven, then?
A: Okay, that'll be fine.

3. A: 여보세요. 영수 있습니까?
B: 전데요. 전화 거는 분은 누구시죠?
A: 나 희영이야.
B: 웬일이야, 희영아?
A: 음, 일간에 만나고 싶어서. 나 곧 캐나다로 유학가게 돼서 한국을 떠날 거야.
B: 오, 그래? 난 그런 줄 몰랐어.
A: 음, 갑작스런 결정이었어.
B: 얼마동안 가 있는데?
A: 약 3년 정도.
B: 그렇게 오래? 난 6시 이후면 언제라도 널 만날 수 있어.
A: 잘됐다. 내일은 어때?
B: 좋아. 어디서 만날까?
A: 7시에 녹색 공원에서 보면 어떨까?
B: 좋아.
A: 그럼 내일 보자.
B: 안녕

4. A: 여보세요. 톰 베이커의 집입니다.
B: 안녕하세요. 베이커씨. 저 박수일입니다. 오늘 저녁 6시쯤 우리 집에서 조촐한 모임을 가지려고 하는데, 오실 수 있겠지요?
A: 누구누구가 오는데요?
B: 저, 사무실에서 같이 근무하는 남자들입니다.
A: 사실, 6시 30분경까지는 무척 바쁠 것 같은데.
B: 그럼 7시로 합시다.
A: 네, 그러면 좋습니다.

5. A: Hello. This is Bill Jameson. May I speak to Anton?

B: Hi. Bill.

A: Hi. What are you doing tonight?

B: Nothing. Why?

A: I thought I'd drop over for a drink or two. We have not seen each other lately.

B: O.K. That's a good idea. What time?

A: How about eight?

B: That's kind of late. Why don't you make it a little earlier?

A: All right. How about seven?

B: That's suits me. Have dinner with us.

A: Well, I didn't mean to invite myself over for dinner.

B: I know. I really want you to come.

A: O.K. If you insist.

B: Great. We'll see you at seven.

A: Bye.

5. A: 여보세요. 저는 빌 제임슨입니다. 앤톤 좀 바꿔주세요.

B: 안녕 빌.

A: 안녕. 너 오늘 밤 뭐 할 일 있어?

B: 아무 일도 없어. 그런데 왜?

A: 그냥 술 한잔 마시러 자네 집에나 갈까 하고 생각했지. 우리는 요즘 통 못 만났잖아.

B: 좋아. 좋은 생각이군. 몇 시에 볼까?

A: 8시 어때?

B: 좀 늦은 것 같군. 조금 일찍 만나면 어때?

A: 좋아. 7시는 어때?

B: 괜찮아. 우리 집에서 함께 식사하도록 해!

A: 음, 난 식사 초대를 받으려고 한 것은 아니었는데….

B: 알아. 난 네가 오기를 진실로 바래.

A: 좋아. 정 그렇다면.

B: 그럼 7시에 보자.

A: 안녕.

C. Important Points

1. 〈의역하면 좋은 문장〉

- You're just the person I'd like to see.
  당신은 내가 보고 싶은(만나고 싶은) 사람이다.
  → 당신을 꼭 만나고 싶은데요.
- on one's mind: 마음에 걸리다
- What's on your mind? 무엇이 당신의 마음에 걸리세요?
  → 무슨 일입니까?
- drop into: -에 잠시 들르다 (=stop by)
- Stop by my house! 우리 집에 잠깐 와!

Yes, I will. 알았어, 그럴게.

2.
- put someone down: 리스트에 -의 이름을 적다

  A: I'm calling about the job interview.
  면접 때문에 전화를 드렸습니다.
  I'm sorry that I can't come to the job interview by 1 o'clock on the 25th. Is it okay if I come by around 2:30?
  죄송하지만 25일날 1시까지 면접하러 못가겠어요. 2시 30분까지 가면 안될까요?

  B: Certainly, I'll put you down for 2:30.
  물론이죠. 2시 30분에 오시는 것으로 기록해 놓겠습니다.
- I'll put your name down for then.
  그 시간으로 선생님의 성함을 적어놓겠습니다.

3. • 유학으로 to study abroad
• 미국 유학 중에 during one's stay in the U.S. as a student
• 국비로 유학하다 study abroad at government expense
• 다년간 해외에서 유학하다 study abroad for a number of years
• 일종의, ~와 같은 것 a sort of
• 얼마동안 가 있을 겁니까? How long will you be gone?
• 그렇게 오래? That long?
• 기뻐서 ~하다. I'll be happy to~
• 내 쪽은 형편이 좋아. Suits me fine.

〈Suit의 다양한 쓰임〉

• suit 원래 뜻은 「뒤따르다, 좇다」의 뜻
1. (뒤따르는 것) → 「한 벌(의 것)」
2. (좇는 것) → (정의를 추구하는 것) → 「소송」
3. (맞추다) → 「어울리다, 잘 맞다」 → 「적합하다」 → 「(형편이) 알맞다」
ex) The five o'clock train suits me fine.
다섯 시 열차면 내게 편리하다.
• suit all tastes 어느 사람에게나 맞다.
• suit one down to the ground 안성맞춤이다.
• suit yourself. 마음대로 하시오, 싫으면 그만두시오.

4. • make it
1. 목표를 달성 하다, (일을) 잘 해내다
2. (약속장소, 시간, 가격 따위를) ~로 하다
3. 제 시간에 대다.
• Why not make it seven, then? 그럼 7시로 합시다
• Okay, then let's make it at seven. 좋습니다. 그럼 7시로 합시다.
• Why not stop[drop] in at seven, then? 그럼 7시에 들르지 그래?
• How does seven o'clock sound? 7시는 어떨까?

5.
- drop over: 느닷없이 가다(미국의 구어체 표현)
- suit: ~에 적합하다, 어울리다.
- We haven't seen each other lately. 우린 요즘 통 만나지 못했잖아.
  cf.) Long time no see. 오랜만이다.
- How about ~ing?혹은 명사: ~하는 게 어때?
  e.g.) How about eight? 8시는 어때?
- If you insist. 만약 네가 그렇게 주장한다면 → 정 그렇다면.

D. Filling in the Blanks

1. A: Hello. A.B.C. Shipping Co.

   B: Yes. This is Mr. Shim Ki-Hyun. ________________ this afternoon?

   A: Let me check, please. Oh, I see Mr. Smith has 20 minutes at 2:30, 30 minutes at 4:00.

   B: ________________ at 2:30?

   A: Surely. I'll put you down for that time.

   B: Thank you.

2. A: Hello. ______________________.

   B: Hi! Mr. Baker. This is Park Soo-Il. I'm having a little get-together over at my place tonight at about six. Will you be able to join us?

   A: ______________________ there?

   B: Oh, just some of the co-workers from the office.

   A: Well, I'll tell you. I'll be pretty tied up until around 6:30 or so.

   B: ____________________ at seven, then?

   A: Okay, that'll be fine.

3. B: How long will you be gone?

   A: ____________________.

   B: That long? Well, I'll be happy to meet you any time after six o'clock.

   A: Excellent. How about tomorrow?

   B: That will be fine. ______________________?

   A: How about the Green Park at seven?

   B: ________________.

   A: All right. See you tomorrow then!

   B: Good-bye.

E. Dictation

1. ______________________________

2. ______________________________

3. ______________________________

4. ______________________________

5. ______________________________

6. ______________________________

7. ______________________________

8. ______________________________

9. ______________________________

10. ______________________________

11. ______________________________

12. ______________________________

13. ______________________________

14. ______________________________

15. ______________________________

E. Dictation 2

1. ______________________________

2. ______________________________

3. ______________________________

4. ______________________________

5. ______________________________

6. ______________________________

7. ______________________________

8. ______________________________

9. ______________________________

10. ______________________________

11. ______________________________

12. ______________________________

13. ______________________________

14. ______________________________

15. ______________________________

PART 1

2. 예약

2-1 호텔예약

A. Dialogue

- Listen to the teacher.
- Repeat after the teacher.
- Practice by yourself.
- Memorize the dialogue.

1. A: Hello, Crown Hotel, May I help you?
   B: Yes, I'd like to book a room please.
   A: When for, sir?
   B: July 3rd.
   A: How long are you going to stay?
   B: A couple of nights.
   A: What kind of room would you like, sir?
   B: A single room with a fine view.
   A: May I have your name, please?
   B: Han-Gyu Lee.
   A: Mr. Lee, a single room with a fine view for the 3rd and the 4th of July.
   B: That's right. Thanks, bye now.
   A: Good bye, sir.

Business English Conversation

B. Practice

- Read through the dialogue in Korean.
- Repeat the dialogue in English.

1. A: 예, 크라운 호텔입니다. 무엇을 도와 드릴까요?
 B: 예, 방을 예약하고 싶은데요.
 A: 원하시는 날짜가 언제죠?
 B: 7월 3일요.
 A: 얼마나 묵으실 거죠?
 B: 이틀이요.
 A: 어떤 방을 원하시죠?
 B: 전망이 좋은 1인 실이요.
 A: 이름을 말씀해 주시겠습니까?
 B: 이한규입니다.
 A: 손님께서는 7월 3, 4 일 경치 좋은 방을 예약하셨습니다.
 B: 예, 맞습니다. 고맙습니다. 그럼.
 A: 안녕히 계십시오.

2. A: Do you have a room for tomorrow night, please?
B: Would that be a single room, ma'am?
A: Yes, a single room.
B: And how long would you be staying?
A: I'd be staying three nights.
B: Three nights. I can give you a single room at a hundred-dollars ($100) a night, including breakfast. Would that be suitable?
A: Yes, that would be fine. My name is Judy Clark - Ms. Judy Clark.
B: Very good, Ms. Clark. We look forward to seeing you.

3. A: I'd like to reserve a room for two, please. We will be arriving on December 8th and stay until the 11th.
B: Very well, sir. We have a double room and also a deluxe suite. Which one would you like?
A: Deluxe suite, please.
B: Okay, who is the booking for?
A: Benjamin Dake.
B: I'm sorry, sir. Could you please spell your full name?
A: B-E-N-J-A-M-I-N D-A-K-E, Benjamin Dake.

2. A: 내일 밤 묵을 방 있나요?

B: 1인실을 찾으시는 건가요. 손님?

A: 네, 1인실이요.

B: 그런데 얼마나 머무실 건데요?

A: 사흘을 묵을 예정입니다.

B: 사흘이라고 하셨죠. 아침 식사를 포함해서 하루에 100불에 1인실을 드릴 수가 있습니다. 괜찮으세요?

A: 네, 좋습니다. 제 이름은 주디 클락, Ms. 주디 클락입니다.

B: 잘 알겠습니다, 클락씨. 뵙게 되기를 고대합니다.

3. A: 두 사람을 위한 방을 예약하고 싶습니다. 우리는 8일날 도착해서 11일까지 묵을 겁니다.

B: 잘 알겠습니다, 손님. 2인실과 대형 객실이 있습니다. 어느 쪽을 원하세요?

A: 대형객실로 하죠.

B: 좋습니다. 예약은 누구 앞으로 하죠?

A: 벤자민 데이크 앞으로 해 주세요.

B: 죄송하지만 손님. 손님 성함의 철자를 불러 주시겠어요?

A: B-E-N-J-A-M-I-N D-A-K-E, 벤자민 데이크입니다.

4. A: Hello, we just arrived in New York.
Do you have any rooms?
B: I'm sorry, we're fully booked.
A: Can you suggest another hotel?
B: There's a nice one right next door.
Would you like me to call for you?
A: I'd really appreciate it. Thank you.
B: Ma'am, they do have a vacancy. Please give me your name and I'll reserve the rooms for you.

5. A: Hello? Is this the Walker Hotel?
B: Yes, it is. May I help you?
A: Yes, I want to reserve a double room with bath for two nights starting tonight.
B: I'm sorry, sir. There are no vacancies tonight.
A: Do you expect any openings tomorrow night?
B: No, not until Saturday, I'm afraid.
A: Oh, I see. Thank you just the same.

4. A: 안녕하세요, 우리는 뉴욕에 막 도착했는데요. 방이 있습니까?

B: 죄송하지만, 빈 방이 없는데요.

A: 다른 호텔 좀 알려 주실 수 없나요?

B: 바로 옆에 훌륭한 호텔이 하나 있어요.
제가 손님을 위해서 전화를 해 드릴까요?

A: 그렇게 해 주신다면 정말 고맙겠어요. 고맙습니다.

B: 손님, 그 호텔에는 방이 있답니다. 성함을 알려 주세요. 그러면 제가 손님을 위해서 예약을 해 드릴게요.

5. A: 여보세요. 거기 워커 호텔입니까?

B: 네, 그렇습니다. 뭘 도와 드릴까요?

A: 네, 오늘밤부터 이틀간 욕실이 딸린 2인용 침대가 있는 방 하나를 예약하고 싶은데요.

B: 죄송합니다, 손님. 오늘밤은 빈 방이 없습니다.

A: 내일 밤엔 빈 방이 있겠습니까?

B: 아니오, 죄송하지만 토요일까지는 없을 것 같은데요.

A: 아, 알겠습니다. 아무튼 감사합니다.

C. Important Points

1.
- May I help you? = Do you need any help? = How can I help you? = What can I do for you?: (무얼) 도와 드릴까요?
- I'd like to make a reservation. =I'd like to reserve a room (방을) 예약하고 싶은데요.
  cf) I have a reservation.: 예약이 되어 있는데요.
- Do you have a vacancy? = Do you have accommodations? = Do you have any rooms available?: 방 있나요?

2.
- 호텔 예약의 경우 많은 경우에 그 다음 날 아침 식사 가격이 포함되는 경우가 많다. 이런 경우 대개 식권 등을 room key와 함께 주는 경우가 많다.
- I can give you a single room at a hundred-dollars ($100) a night, including breakfast.
  아침 식사를 포함해서 하루에 100불에 1인실을 드릴 수가 있습니다.

3.
- suite room: 침실에 거실, 주방, 욕실 등이 갖춰진 대형 객실을 의미함. 발음에 주의해야 하는데 많은 한국인들이 이것을 [수-트]라고 발음하는데 이렇게 발음하면 'suit: 신사복 한벌'의 발음이 되므로 주의해야 한다. 맞는 발음은 [스위-트]라고 해야 한다. 이 발음은 'sweet: 단, 감미로운'의 발음과 같다.
- Who is the booking for?: 예약은 누구를 위한 것이죠?
  → 예약은 누구 앞으로 하죠?

4.
- fully booked: 빈 방이 없다.
- I'd really appreciate it.: 그렇게 해 주신다면 정말 고맙겠습니다.
- vacancy: 빈 방

5. 〈빈 방과 관련된 표현〉

- I'm sorry, sir. There are no vacancies tonight.:
  죄송합니다, 손님. 저녁엔 빈 방이 없습니다.
- 빈 방: opening(s), vacancies, any rooms open, any rooms available
- 내일은 빈 방이 나올까요?
  Do you expect any openings tomorrow night?
  Do you expect any available rooms[rooms available] tomorrow?
  Are there any rooms open tomorrow?
  Will you have anything tomorrow then?
  Do you have anything available?
- 내일은 예약이 가능합니까?
  Is it possible to make a reservation for tomorrow?
  Can I make a booking for tomorrow night?

D. Filling in the Blanks

1. A: Hello, Crown Hotel, May I help you?
   B: Yes, ________________________ please.
   A: When for, sir?
   B: July 3rd.
   A: How long are you going to stay?
   B: ________________________.
   A: What kind of room would you like, sir?
   B: A single room with a fine view.

2. A: Hello, we just arrived in New York.
   Do you have any rooms?
   B: I'm sorry, ________________________.
   A: Can you suggest another hotel?
   B: There's a nice one right next door.
   Would you like me to call for you?
   A: ________________________. Thank you.
   B: Ma'am, ________________________. Please give me your name and I'll reserve the rooms for you.

3. A: Hello? Is this the Walker Hotel?
   B: Yes, it is. May I help you?
   A: Yes, I want to ____________________ with bath for two nights starting tonight.
   B: I'm sorry, sir. There are ________________________.
   A: Do you expect ____________________ tomorrow night?
   B: No, not until Saturday, I'm afraid.
   A: Oh, I see. Thank you just the same.

E. Dictation

1. ______________________________

2. ______________________________

3. ______________________________

4. ______________________________

5. ______________________________

6. ______________________________

7. ______________________________

8. ______________________________

9. ______________________________

10. ______________________________

11. ______________________________

12. ______________________________

13. ______________________________

14. ______________________________

15. ______________________________

2-2 비행기예약

A. Dialogue

- Listen to the teacher.
- Repeat after the teacher.
- Practice by yourself.
- Memorize the dialogue.

1. A: Hello, KAL Airlines.
   B: Yes, I'd like to make a reservation for a flight to Seoul.
   A: When would you like the reservation for, sir?
   B: The day after tomorrow, if possible.
   A: All right, sir. We have one flight leaving at 11:00 a.m. and another at 6:00 p.m.
   B: Please book me for the 6 o'clock flight.

2. A: Hello, I'd like to reconfirm my reservation.
   B: May I have your name, please?
   A: Mr. Jin-Soo Kim.
   B: May I ask what reservation you're holding?
   A: Flight 505 leaving tomorrow at 9:20 p.m. to New York.
   B: Hold on, please. Yes, you're booked on our flight 207 to New York tomorrow.

B. Practice

- Read through the dialogue in Korean.
- Repeat the dialogue in English.

1. A: 여보세요. KAL 항공입니다.
   B: 네, 서울행 비행기표를 예약하고 싶은데요.
   A: 언제 날짜로 예약하시겠습니까?
   B: 가능하면 모레요.
   A: 좋습니다. 오전 열한시 비행기와 오후 여섯시 비행기가 있는데요.
   B: 여섯시 비행기로 해 주십시오.

2. A: 여보세요, 예약 재확인을 하려고 합니다.
   B: 성함이 어떻게 되십니까?
   A: 김진수입니다.
   B: 예약 내용이 무엇입니까?
   A: 내일 오후 9시 20분발 뉴욕행 505 비행기입니다.
   B: 잠깐만 기다려 주십시오. 네, 내일 뉴욕행 505호기로 예약이 되어 있습니다.

3. A: Northwest Airlines. May I help you?

B: My name is D. S. Park. I have a reservation for tomorrow morning on flight 735 to Washington.

A: Just a minute, please. (later). Yes, your reservation has been confirmed, sir.

B: I'd like to change my reservation, if I may.

A: When would you like to go?

B: I'd like to leave on the afternoon flight.

A: That would be flight 738. We have seats available on that flight.

B: Good. I'll take that one, then.

4. A: Thai Airlines. Sue speaking. May I help you?

B: Yes, I'd like to get a seat to Bangkok tomorrow.

A: O.K. No problem. Business class or economy class, sir?

B: Business class, please.

A: May I have your name and phone number, please?

B: Peter Powell. 381-273-5712.

5. A: I'd like to make a booking for a flight to Brisbane and Sydney.

B: Okay, sir. We have a direct flight to Brisbane, and we can book you all the way through to Sydney without any delay.

A: I'm not sure how long I'll stay in Brisbane, so please leave it open.

B: Okay, sir, we'll leave that open for you.

A: How about my baggage? Can that be checked all the way through to Sydney?

B: No, sir. You'll have to pick it up in Brisbane and recheck it through after you decide which flight you're taking to Sydney.

3. A: 노스웨스트 항공입니다. 뭘 도와 드릴까요?
B: 제 이름은 디 · 에스 박입니다. 내일 아침 워싱턴행 735호기를 예약했는데요.
A: 잠깐만 기다려 주십시오. (잠시 후). 네, 예약하신 것 확인됐습니다.
B: 가능하다면 예약을 좀 바꾸고 싶은데요.
A: 언제로 하시겠습니까?
B: 오후 비행기로 떠났으면 하는데요.
A: 738호기가 되겠군요. 그 비행기편에 좌석이 있습니다.
B: 좋습니다. 그러면 그걸로 하겠습니다.

4. A: 타이항공 수입니다. 뭘 도와드릴까요?
B: 네, 내일 방콕으로 가는 표를 사고 싶습니다.
A: 좋습니다. 그렇게 하겠습니다. 비즈니스석으로 드릴까요, 혹은 이코노미석으로 드릴까요, 손님?
B: 1등석으로 주세요.
A: 성함과 전화번호를 알려 주시겠습니까?
B: 피터 파월이고요. 전화번호는 381-273-5712입니다.

5. A: 브리즈번 경유 시드니행 비행기를 예약했으면 합니다.
B: 브리즈번까지 바로 가는 비행기가 있습니다. 그리고 시드니까지 지체 없이 타고 가실 수 있도록 예약해 드리겠습니다.
A: 브리즈번에서 며칠이나 머물지 잘 모릅니다. 그러니까 무예약으로 해 주십시오.
B: 알겠습니다. 무예약으로 해드리겠습니다.
A: 짐은 어떻게 되지요? 시드니까지 곧장 탁송됩니까?
B: 아닙니다. 브리즈번에서 짐을 찾으셨다가 시드니행 항공편을 결정하신 뒤에 다시 부치셔야 합니다.

C. Important Points

1. 〈비행기 예약을 위해 쓰는 표현〉

- I'd like to make a reservation for a flight to Seoul.:
  서울행 비행기를 예약하고자 합니다.
- I'd like to fly to Seoul on the 15th.:
  15일 비행기로 서울을 가고자 합니다.
- I'd like to make a flight[plane] reservation for Seoul on May 10th.
  5월 10일 서울가는 비행기를 예약하고자 합니다.
- Can I make a reservation for June 5th on KE 322?
  6월 5일의 KE 322편의 예약을 할 수가 있습니까?
- Would it be possible to get a flight to Seoul the 9th?
  9일날 서울행 비행기 예약이 가능할까요?
- I'd like a ticket for one to Tokyo.
  동경행 비행기 표 한 장이 필요합니다.
- I'd like to book a flight to New York.
  뉴욕행 비행기를 예약하려고 합니다.
- Will you put me on the waiting list?
  대기자 명단에 올려 주시겠습니까?

2. 〈예약의 확인〉

예약의 확인이란 비행기를 타겠다는 연락을 다신 한 번 취하는 일이다. 미국, 영국, 캐나다 등지에서는 실제로 비행기에 탑승하기 3일(72시간) 이전에 예약의 확인을 하지 않으면 안되게 되어 있다.

- I'd like to confirm my reservation.: 예약을 확인하고 싶습니다.
- I want to confirm my flight.: 내 비행기편을 확인하고 싶습니다.
- I'd like to check on my reservation.: 예약을 확인하고 싶습니다.
- We've confirmed your seat.: 좌석이 확인되었습니다.

- We haven't been able to confirm your reservation.
  예약을 확인할 수가 없습니다.
- We have you on stand-by.
  예약이 불가능해서 대기 리스트에 올려놨습니다.

3. 〈비행기 예약 문답〉

- When would you like to go?: 몇 시 비행기를 원하세요?
- 오후에 출발하는 비행기였으면 좋겠습니다.
  I'd like to leave on the afternoon flight.
  I'd like to take the afternoon flight.
  I'd like to fly in the afternoon if there are any flights avavilable then.

4.

- open: 항공기 번호와 탑승시간은 미정으로 해두고 예약을 하는 것.
- I'm not sure how long I'll stay in Chicago. So please leave it open.
  시카고에서 얼마동안 머물지 아직 잘 모릅니다. 그러니까 미정으로 [무예 약으로] 해두세요.
- Would you care to leave it open?
  그 사항은 미정으로 해두시겠습니까?
- I don't know now. Just leave it open.
  지금은 모르겠습니다. 그냥 무예약으로 해주십시오.
- I have an open ticket. Do you have any seats available on the next flight to New York?
  비행편 번호와 시각이 미정인 항공권을 가지고 있습니다. 차기 뉴욕행 항공편에 좌석이 있습니까?

D. Filling in the Blanks

1. A: Hello, I'd like to ______________________.
   B: May I have your name, please?
   A: Mr. Jin-Soo Kim.
   B: May I ask ______________________?
   A: Flight 505 leaving tomorrow at 9:20 p.m. to New York.
   B: Hold on, please. Yes, ____________ on our flight 207 to New York tomorrow.

2. A: Northwest Airlines. May I help you?
   B: My name is D. S. Park. ________________ for tomorrow morning on flight 735 to Washington.
   A: Just a minute, please. (later). Yes, your reservation has been confirmed, sir.
   B: I'd like to ________________, if I may.
   A: When would you like to go?
   B: I'd like to leave on the afternoon flight.
   A: That would be flight 738. We ________________ on that flight.
   B: Good. I'll take that one, then.

3. A: I'd like to ________________for a flight to Brisbane and Sydney.
   B: Okay, sir. We have a direct flight to Brisbane, and we can book you ________________ to Sydney without any delay.
   A: I'm not sure how long I'll stay in Brisbane, so please leave it open.
   B: Okay, sir, we'll leave that open for you.
   A: ________________? Can that be checked all the way through to Sydney?
   B: No, sir. You'll have to pick it up in Brisbane and recheck it through after you decide which flight you're taking to Sydney.

E. Dictation

1. ______________________________

2. ______________________________

3. ______________________________

4. ______________________________

5. ______________________________

6. ______________________________

7. ______________________________

8. ______________________________

9. ______________________________

10. ______________________________

11. ______________________________

12. ______________________________

13. ______________________________

14. ______________________________

15. ______________________________

2-3 식당예약

A. Dialogue

- Listen to the teacher.
- Repeat after the teacher.
- Practice by yourself.
- Memorize the dialogue.

1. A: Hello. Can you tell me what your hours are?
   B: Yes. We are open from 10 a.m. till 11 p.m.
   A: How about Saturday?
   B: We are open until midnight. We are closed all day Monday.
   A: Is a reservation necessary?
   B: Yes.
   A: I would like to make reservations for tomorrow night, at six o'clock, for four. We would like a table by the window.
   B: May I have your name, please?
   A: Jameson Smith.
   B: How do you spell it?
   A: That's J-a-m-e-s-o-n S-m-i-t-h.
   B: I see. Thank you.
   A: Thank you.

2. A: Please reserve a table for two at seven tonight.
   B: Yes, sir. Your name and phone number, please.
   A: My name is Jim Pate and my phone number is 397-2781.
   I'd like a table near the window, please.
   B: I'll try.
   A: Do you require a coat and tie?
   B: It would be appreciated.

B. Practice

- Read through the dialogue in Korean.
- Repeat the dialogue in English.

1. A: 여보세요. 거기 영업시간을 알려 주세요.
   B: 오전 10 시부터 오후 11 시까지 입니다.
   A: 토요일은 어떻습니까?
   B: 자정까지 엽니다. 월요일에는 쉽니다.
   A: 예약이 필요합니까?
   B: 네
   A: 내일 밤 6시에 4명을 예약하고 싶습니다. 창가 쪽 자리로 해주세요.
   B: 성함을 말씀해 주시겠습니까?
   A: 제임슨 스미스입니다.
   B: 철자가 어떻게 되지요?
   A: J-a-m-e-s-o-n S-m-i-t-h입니다.
   B: 알았습니다. 감사합니다.
   A: 감사합니다.

2. A: 오늘 밤 7시에 두명을 위해 자리를 예약해 주세요.
   B: 네, 손님. 손님의 성함과 전화번호를 알려 주세요.
   A: 내 이름은 짐 페이트이고 전화번호는 397-2781이에요.
   창가 가까운 자리를 원합니다.
   B: 노력해 보겠습니다.
   A: 정장을 입어야 합니까?
   B: 그렇게 해 주신다면 감사하겠습니다.

3. A: Good afternoon, this is Mr. Lee. May I help you?

B: Yes, is this the Steak House?

A: Yes, it is. What can I do for you?

B: I want to reserve a table for dinner tonight. Do you have an opening?

A: Yes, we have. Please give your name and the number of guests.

B: Thomas Moore, party of four. We would like a table by the window if possible.

A: Certainly, we will reserve a table by the window. What time will you be here?

B: 6 p.m.

A: What is your phone number?

B: It's 782-3782.

A: We look forward to seeing you.

4. A: Is a reservation necessary for dinner?

B: Yes, sir.

A: Can I reserve three seats for 7 tomorrow evening?

B: Yes, you can.

A: May I ask you to reserve a nice table for us?

B: Of course, sir. Could I ask your name and phone number, please?

3. A: 안녕하세요. 저는 이입니다. 뭘 도와드릴까요?
B: 네, 이 집이 스테이크 하우스인가요?
A: 네, 맞습니다. 뭘 해드릴까요?
B: 오늘 저녁 식사를 위해 예약을 하고 싶은데요. 자리가 있나요?
A: 네, 있습니다. 손님의 성함과 오실 손님 수를 알려 주시죠.
B: 토마스 무어구요. 4명입니다. 가능하면 창가 자리로 하고 싶습니다.
A: 물론 창가 쪽으로 해드리겠습니다. 이곳에 몇시에 오실 건가요?
B: 6시에 오겠습니다.
A: 전화번호가 어떻게 되시죠?
B: 782-3782입니다.
A: 기다리고 있겠습니다.

4. A: 저녁식사를 위해서 자리를 예약하는 것이 필요한가요?
B: 네, 손님.
A: 내일 저녁 7시에 세 자리를 예약할 수 있을까요?
B: 네, 그렇습니다.
A: 좋은 자리를 예약해 주실 수 있으세요?
B: 물론이죠, 손님. 손님 성함과 전화번호를 알려 주시겠어요?

5. A: This is the Seoul Buffet, Judy speaking. May I help you?

B: Yes, do you have a dinner buffet?

A: Yes, we do.

B: I want to make a dinner reservation for tomorrow at 7 p.m.
Do you have a quiet corner?

A: Yes, we do.
How many in your party?

B: About ten people.

A: I see. What time will you be here?

B: We should arrive between six thirty and seven.

A: Would you give me the name and phone number?

B: James Miller, 765-2375.

A: Thank you.

B: What is the price?

A: It's 20,000 Won per person, including tax.

5. A: 서울 뷔페입니다. 전 쥬디이고요. 뭘 도와 드릴까요?

B: 저녁 뷔페를 하나요?

A: 네, 그렇습니다.

B: 내일 저녁 7시에 저녁 예약을 하고 싶은데요. 조용한 자리가 있습니까?

A: 네, 그렇습니다. 일행이 몇 분이나 되시죠?

B: 약 10명 정도 됩니다.

A: 알겠습니다. 여기에 몇 시에 오실 겁니까?

B: 6시 30분에서 7시 사이에 도착할 겁니다.

A: 성함과 전화번호를 알려 주시겠어요?

B: 제임스 밀러이고 765-2375입니다.

A: 고맙습니다.

B: 값이 얼마죠?

A: 세금을 포함해서 개인당 20,000원입니다.

C. Important Points

1. • We are open from 10 a.m. till 11 p.m.
   오전 10 시부터 오후 11시까지 엽니다.
   • We would like a table by the window.: 창가 쪽 자리로 해주세요.

2. • Do you require a coat and tie?: 외투와 넥타이를 요구하십니까?
   → 정장을 입어야 합니까?

3. • opening: 빈 좌석
   • We look forward to seeing you.: 기다리고 있겠습니다.

4. • Is a reservation necessary for dinner?
   저녁식사를 위해서 자리를 예약하는 것이 필요한가요?
   • May I ask you to reserve a nice table for us?
   좋은 자리를 예약해 주실 수 있으세요?

5. • party: 일행
   • How many in your party?: 일행이 몇 분이나 되시죠?

D. Filling in the Blanks

1. A: Please ______________________ at seven tonight.
   B: Yes, sir. Your name and phone number, please.
   A: My name is Jim Pate and my phone number is 397-2781.
   I'd like a table near the window, please.
   B: I'll try.
   A: ______________________?
   B: It would be appreciated.

2. A: Good afternoon, this is Mr. Lee. May I help you?
   B: Yes, is this the Steak House?
   A: Yes, it is. __________________ for you?
   B: I want to reserve a table for dinner tonight. ________________?
   A: Yes, we have. Please give your name and the number of guests.
   B: Thomas Moore, party of four. We would like ________________
   if possible.
   A: Certainly, we will reserve a table by the window. What time will
   you be here?
   B: 6 p.m.

3. A: Is ______________________ for dinner?
   B: Yes, sir.
   A: Can I reserve three seats for 7 tomorrow evening?
   B: Yes, you can.
   A: May I ask you to reserve a nice table for us?
   B: ________________. Could I ask your name and phone number,
   please?

E. Dictation

1. ______________________________

2. ______________________________

3. ______________________________

4. ______________________________

5. ______________________________

6. ______________________________

7. ______________________________

8. ______________________________

9. ______________________________

10. ______________________________

11. ______________________________

12. ______________________________

13. ______________________________

14. ______________________________

15. ______________________________

E. Dictation 2

1. ______________________________

2. ______________________________

3. ______________________________

4. ______________________________

5. ______________________________

6. ______________________________

7. ______________________________

8. ______________________________

9. ______________________________

10. ______________________________

11. ______________________________

12. ______________________________

13. ______________________________

14. ______________________________

15. ______________________________

2-4 공연예약

A. Dialogue

- Listen to the teacher.
- Repeat after the teacher.
- Practice by yourself.
- Memorize the dialogue.

1. A: Two adults for 'Cats' for the twelve o'clock show, please.
B: I'm sorry, but the show has just been sold out.
A: Oh, really? what about the next show?
B: How about the three o'clock show?
A: That's fine. Two adults, please.
B: Seven dollars each. The total amount is fourteen dollars.
A: Here is twenty dollars.
B: Thank you. Your tickets and the change, six dollars.
A: Thanks a lot.

2. A: One adult for 'Star wars', please.
B: I'm sorry, but the show for today has been sold out.
A: Oh, really? Then, how about 'Last Christmas'?
B: We have some tickets for the show.
A: One for the seven o'clock show, please.
B: Seven fifty.
A: O.K. Here it is.
B: Thank you.

B. Practice

- Read through the dialogue in Korean.
- Repeat the dialogue in English.

1. A: 12시 공연 'Cats' 어른표 2장 주세요.
   B: 죄송하지만 12시 것은 매진되었는데요.
   A: 아, 그래요? 다음 공연은 어때요?
   B: 3시 공연은 어떻습니까?
   A: 좋습니다. 어른표 2장 주세요.
   B: 일인 당 7달러입니다. 총 14달러입니다.
   A: 여기 20달러 있습니다.
   B: 고맙습니다. 여기 표와 거스름돈 6달러입니다.
   A: 대단히 고맙습니다.

2. A: '스타워즈' 어른표 하나 주세요.
   B: 죄송합니다만 오늘 상영은 매진되었습니다.
   A: 아, 정말입니까? 그러면 '라스트 크리스마스'는 어떻습니까?
   B: 그것에 대한 표는 좀 있습니다.
   A: 7시 상영표로 하나 주세요.
   B: 7달러 50센트입니다.
   A: 좋습니다. 여기 있습니다.
   B: 고맙습니다.

3. A: Excuse me. How much is the admission?

B: Five dollars.

A: Is there a student discount?

B: Yes, students tickets are three dollars with ID.

A: Good, let me have two student tickets.

B: May I see your student ID, please?

A: Yes, here you are.

4. A: Hello. Do you have tickets available for today's performance?

B: Yes, we do have a few left.

A: For which performance?

B: The 8 p.m. performance.

A: Could I make reservations by telephone?

B: Sure.

A: I would like four "S" tickets, please.

B: There are only two "S" tickets available.

A: Well··· What do you have available?

B: Seats on the balcony.

A: Fine, I would like four tickets for the 8 p.m. performance.

B: Could I get you anything else?

A: No, thanks. That's all for now.

3. A: 죄송합니다만 입장권이 얼마죠?
B: 5달러입니다.
A: 학생에게 할인이 있나요?
B: 네, 학생표는 학생증을 제시하는 경우에 3달러입니다.
A: 좋아요, 학생표 2장 주세요.
B: 학생증 좀 보여 주시겠어요?
A: 네, 여기 있습니다.

4. A: 여보세요. 오늘 공연 표 아직 있습니까?
B: 네, 조금 남아 있습니다.
A: 몇 시 공연입니까?
B: 오후 8시 공연입니다.
A: 전화로 예약 할 수 있습니까?
B: 물론입니다.
A: S석으로 4장 주십시오.
B: 두 장 밖에 없습니다.
A: 그럼… 어느 자리가 비어 있습니까?
B: 2층석이 비어 있습니다.
A: 그럼, 저녁 8시 공연 티켓 4장 주세요.
B: 다른 것 필요 하신 거 있으십니까?
A: 아닙니다. 지금은 이것으로 됐습니다.

5. A: May I help you?

B: Yes, I'd like to have tickets for Soo-Mi Cho's concert at the Opera House.

A: How many tickets do you need?

B: Three adults.

A: O.K. July 7th and 8th are on sale now.

B: What section would you like? Most of the good seats are sold out but we still have some balcony seats left.

A: I will take three balcony seats for July 7th. How much are they?

B: Seventy-five dollars. How would you like to pay for these tickets?

A: By cash.

B: Here you are. Thank you.

5. A: 뭘 도와드릴까요?

B: 네, 오페라 하우스에서의 조수미씨 음악회표를 사고 싶은데요.

A: 표가 몇 장이나 필요하시죠?

B: 성인으로 3장이요.

A: 좋습니다. 7월 7일과 8일 표를 판매 중입니다.

B: 어떤 구역표를 원하세요? 대부분의 좋은 자리는 다 팔렸습니다. 하지만 2층 좌석은 좀 남아 있습니다.

A: 7월 7일자 2층 좌석으로 3장을 구입하겠습니다. 얼마죠?

B: 75달러입니다. 돈은 어떻게 지불하시겠습니까?

A: 현금으로 드리죠.

B: (표) 여기 있습니다. 고맙습니다.

C. Important Points

1. • sold out: 매진된
   • change: 거스름돈

2. • how about-: -는 어떻습니까?
   • Here it is = Here you are: 여기 있습니다.

3. • ID (=identification): 신분증. 주민등록증, 운전면허증, 학생증 등이 여기에 해당된다.

4. **〈공연 입장권 예매 표현〉**
   • 매진입니다: It is sold out.
   • 지금 어떤 공연을 하고 있습니까?: Do you know what is playing?
   • 리어 왕을 공연하고 있습니다.: It is playing King Lear.
   • 그 표를 주세요.: I'll take that.
   • 며칠까지 공연 합니까?: How long will this performance be showing?

5. • balcony seat: (극장의) 2층 좌석
   • orchestra seat: 아래층 무대 전면 좌석
   • How would you like to pay for these tickets?
   (이 표들에 대한) 요금은 어떻게 지불하시겠습니까?

D. Filling in the Blanks

1. A: __________________ 'Cats' for the twelve o'clock show, please.
   B: I'm sorry, but the show has just been sold out.
   A: Oh, really? what about the next show?
   B: How about the three o'clock show?
   A: That's fine. Two adults, please.
   B: Seven dollars each. ____________________ fourteen dollars.
   A: Here is twenty dollars.
   B: Thank you. Your tickets and the change, six dollars.
   A: Thanks a lot.

2. A: One adult for 'Star wars', please.
   B: I'm sorry, but the show for today __________________.
   A: Oh, really? Then, how about 'Last Christmas'?
   B: We have some tickets for the show.
   A: One __________________________, please.
   B: Seven fifty.
   A: O.K. Here it is.
   B: Thank you.

3. A: Excuse me. ______________________________?
   B: Five dollars.
   A: Is there ______________________?
   B: Yes, students tickets are three dollars with ID.
   A: Good, let me have two student tickets.
   B: May I see your student ID, please?
   A: Yes, ____________________.

E. Dictation

1. ____________________

2. ____________________

3. ____________________

4. ____________________

5. ____________________

6. ____________________

7. ____________________

8. ____________________

9. ____________________

10. ____________________

11. ____________________

12. ____________________

13. ____________________

14. ____________________

15. ____________________

E. Dictation 2

1. ______________________________

2. ______________________________

3. ______________________________

4. ______________________________

5. ______________________________

6. ______________________________

7. ______________________________

8. ______________________________

9. ______________________________

10. ______________________________

11. ______________________________

12. ______________________________

13. ______________________________

14. ______________________________

15. ______________________________

PART I

3. 안내

3-1 물건구입

A. Dialogue

- Listen to the teacher.
- Repeat after the teacher.
- Practice by yourself.
- Memorize the dialogue.

1. A: Excuse me. I'm looking for a gift for my husband.
   B: Did you have anything particular in mind?
   A: Well, every year I get him a tie so I want to give him a different present this year.
   B: How about these leather gloves? They are very popular this year.
   A: Yes, they look very nice. And the price is very reasonable.
   B: They come in a variety of colors and sizes.
   A: Well, I want to take a look at a few more stores before I decide. What are your hours?
   B: We're open from 10 a.m. to 9 p.m.

2. A: How much is this dress?
   B: It's $300.
   A: That's awfully expensive. Can't you come down just a bit more?
   B: Sorry. $300 is as low as I go.
   A: What about that dress over there?
   B: That's even more expensive. That's $350.

Business English Conversation

B. Practice

- Read through the dialogue in Korean.
- Repeat the dialogue in English.

1. A: 실례합니다. 남편을 위한 선물을 사려고 해요.
B: 특별히 생각하고 계신 게 있나요?
A: 음, 매년 넥타이를 해 줬는데 올해는 다른 선물을 주고 싶어요.
B: 이 가죽 장갑이 어때요? 올해는 아주 유행이거든요.
A: 네, 매우 좋아 보이는군요. 그리고 가격도 아주 적당하고요.
B: 색상과 크기도 아주 다양합니다.
A: 음, 결정하기 전에 몇 군데 더 돌아보고 싶군요. 영업시간이 어떻게 됩니까?
B: 아침 10시부터 밤 9시까지 엽니다.

2. A: 이 드레스는 얼마죠?
B: 300달럽니다.
A: 굉장히 비싸군요. 약간만 더 깎아 줄 수 없나요?
B: 죄송합니다. 300달러는 제가 해 드릴 수 있는 가장 낮은 가격입니다.
A: 저 쪽에 있는 드레스는 어때요?
B: 그건 더 비싸요. 350달러입니다.

3. A: Hi, do you need some help?

B: Yes, do you have that dress in blue?

A: Oh, the one in the display window? Yes, we do. Do you wear a medium?

B: Yes, I do. Can I try it on?

A: Sure, the fitting rooms are at the back of the store.

B: How many items can I take in at one time?

A: Only three at a time.

4. A: Can I help you ma'am?

B: Yes, I want to return this watch I bought last week.

A: Why are you returning it?

B: This watch is slow.

A: Do you have your sales receipt?

B: Yes, here you are.

A: Do you want to exchange it for another one or return it for a refund?

B: I would like to have a refund on it.

5. A: Excuse me. I bought this sweater for my nephew, but he is allergic to wool. I'd like to exchange this for something else.

B: That'll be fine. Why don't you take a look around?

A: I notice that you have very few items left in a size 7.

B: Yes, but in two weeks we're getting a shipment of the new fall collection for kids.

A: Then, I'll wait until then to exchange this sweater.

3. A: 안녕하세요, 도움이 필요하신가요?
B: 네, 저 옷으로 푸른색이 있나요?
A: 진열장에 있는 옷이요? 네, 있습니다. 중간 크기를 입으시나요?
B: 네, 그래요. 입어봐도 될까요?
A: 물론이죠, 탈의실은 가게 뒤쪽에 있습니다.
B: 한 번에 몇 벌이나 갖고 들어갈 수 있나요?
A: 한 번에 세 벌입니다.

4. A: 뭘 도와드릴까요, 손님?
B: 네, 지난주에 산 이 시계를 반품하고 싶어요.
A: 왜 반품하는 거죠?
B: 이 시계가 늦게 가거든요.
A: 판매 영수증이 있으세요?
B: 네, 여기 있습니다.
A: 그걸 다른 것과 교환하기를 원하세요, 혹은 반품하고 환불을 받기를 원하세요?
B: 환불받기를 원해요.

5. A: 실례합니다. 조카를 주려고 이 스웨터를 샀는데 그 애가 모직물에 알레르기가 있어요. 이걸 다른 걸로 교환을 하고 싶어요.
B: 그렇게 하시죠. 한 번 돌아보시지 그러세요.
A: 7 사이즈로는 물건이 거의 없는 것 같은데요.
B: 네, 하지만 2주 후에는 아동용 가을 신상품이 들어올 겁니다.
A: 그러면 이 스웨터를 교환하기 위해 그 때까지 기다릴게요.

C. Important Points

1.
- What are your hours?: 영업시간이 어떻게 됩니까?
- take a look at = look at: 보다
- They come in a variety of colors and sizes: 색상과 크기가 아주 다양합니다.

2.
- come down: 값을 내리다
- Can't you come down just a bit more?: 약간만 더 깎아줄 수 없나요?

3.
- Do you have that dress in blue?: 저 옷으로 푸른색이 있습니까?
- display window: 진열장
- try on: 입어보다

4.
- return: 반품하다.
- refund: 환불하다

5.
- shipment: 선적, 수송, 발송
- I'd like to exchange this for something else.: 이걸 다른 걸로 교환을 하고 싶어요.

D. Filling in the Blanks

1. A: Excuse me. I'm looking for a gift for my husband.

   B: Did you have ____________________?

   A: Well, every year I get him a tie so I want to give him a different present this year.

   B: How about these leather gloves? They are very popular this year.

   A: Yes, ____________________. And the price is very reasonable.

   B: They come in ____________________ and sizes.

   A: Well, I want to take a look at a few more stores before I decide. What are your hours?

   B: We're open from 10 a.m. to 9 p.m.

2. A: Hi, do you need some help?

   B: Yes, do you have that dress in blue?

   A: Oh, the one ____________________? Yes, we do. Do you wear a medium?

   B: Yes, I do. ____________________?

   A: Sure, the fitting rooms are at the back of the store.

   B: How many items can I take in at one time?

   A: ____________________.

3. A: Excuse me. I bought this sweater for my nephew, but he is allergic to wool. I'd like to ____________________ for something else.

   B: That'll be fine. ____________________ take a look around?

   A: I notice that you have very few items left in a size 7.

   B: Yes, but in two weeks we're getting a shipment of the new fall collection for kids.

   A: Then, I'll wait until then ____________________.

E. Dictation

1. ______________________________

2. ______________________________

3. ______________________________

4. ______________________________

5. ______________________________

6. ______________________________

7. ______________________________

8. ______________________________

9. ______________________________

10. ______________________________

11. ______________________________

12. ______________________________

13. ______________________________

14. ______________________________

15. ______________________________

E. Dictation 2

1. ______________________________

2. ______________________________

3. ______________________________

4. ______________________________

5. ______________________________

6. ______________________________

7. ______________________________

8. ______________________________

9. ______________________________

10. ______________________________

11. ______________________________

12. ______________________________

13. ______________________________

14. ______________________________

15. ______________________________

3-2 음식관련 대화

A. Dialogue

- Listen to the teacher.
- Repeat after the teacher.
- Practice by yourself.
- Memorize the dialogue.

1. A: May I take your order?
   B: Do you have any specials?
   A: Yes, today's special is linguini with clams.
   B: And what comes with that?
   A: Well, you have a choice of soup or salad.
   B: Okay. I'll have the special with a soup, please.
   A: What kind of dressing would you like on your salad?
   B: I'll have the French dressing.

2. A: May I have some Ginseng tea? My friend says Ginseng is good for my health.
   B: That's right. It's common knowledge in Korea that Ginseng is good for the organs and circulation.
   A: And I want to know where I can buy fresh Ginseng and its products.
   B: You can buy it at the Duty Free shop in front of our restaurant. They have a section specializing in Ginseng and traditional remedies.
   A: O.K. I'll go and see what they are selling.

B. Practice

- Read through the dialogue in Korean.
- Repeat the dialogue in English.

1. A: 주문하시겠습니까?
B: 오늘 특별 요리가 있어요?
A: 네, 오늘의 특별 요리는 대합조개가 들어간 링귀니입니다.
B: 어떤 음식이 함께 나오죠?
A: 스프나 샐러드를 선택하실 수 있습니다.
B: 좋습니다. 특별 요리와 스프를 먹겠습니다.
A: 샐러드에 어떤 종류의 드레싱을 얹으시겠습니까?
B: 프렌치 드레싱을 넣을게요.

2. A: 인삼차 되나요? 친구가 말하기를 건강에 좋다고 하던데요.
B: 네 손님. 한국에서는 인삼차가 인체내의 여러 장기와 혈액 순환에 좋다고 합니다.
A: 신선한 인삼이나 인삼제품 같은 것은 어디서 살 수 있는지 알고 싶습니다.
B: 바로 앞 면세점에서도 살 수 있습니다. 면세점 내에 인삼과 전통 한약제 등이 있는 섹션이 있습니다.
A: 좋습니다. 가서 뭘 파는지 봐야겠네요.

3. A: Hey, something smells good! What are you cooking?
B: Macaroni and Cheese. I hope you like it.
This is a new recipe.
A: Can I try a bit? I promise not to eat too much!
B: Only if you hand me that skillet over there, and then wait. It's still not cooked properly.
A: I think I can do that. Gee, what has that sauce got in it?
B: A little bit of this, and a little bit of that.
I fried some onions and garlic together with some olive oil, then grated some cheese in and left it to cook.
It'll be ready in 10 minutes.
A: I can't wait! My mouth is watering!

4. A: Excuse me, we are ready to order now.
B: All right sir, what would you like?
A: I'll start with a large bowl of clam chowder. And then, the seafood platter with French fries.
B: And ma'am?
C: I'll have the same.
B: Would you like anything to drink with that?
A: Yes, a glass of lemonade.
C: Make that two glasses, please.

5. A: Excuse me. This is your order.
B: Thank you.
A: Would you like anything else?
B: I'd like some more coffee, please.
A: Sure. Enjoy your meal.
……
A: How was your meal?
B: It was good.
A: Would you like some dessert?
B: No, I'm full.

3. A: 냄새가 아주 좋은데! 뭘 요리하고 있어?
B: 마카로니와 치즈야. 좋아하길 바라. 이건 새 요리법이거든.
A: 약간만 맛 좀 볼까? 너무 많이 먹지 않도록 할게!
B: 저기 프라이팬만 내게 건네준다면 먹게 해 줄게, 그런데 좀 기다려. 아직 다 익지 않았거든.
A: 그렇게 해줄 수 있지. 그 소스 안에 뭐가 들어있지?
B: 이것, 저것 조금씩 넣었어. 올리브기름에 양파와 마늘을 같이 넣고 볶은 후에 치즈를 갈아 넣고 좀 더 익히면 돼. 10분 후면 될 거야.
A: 기다리지 못하겠어. 군침이 도는군!

4. A: 저기요, 지금 주문할게요.
B: 좋습니다, 손님. 뭘 드시겠습니까?
A: 조개 삽탕요리 대를 우선 갖다 주세요. 그리고 해산물 접시요리와 채 썬 감자튀김을 갖다 주세요.
B: 그리고 손님은요?
C: 같은 걸로 먹을게요.
B: 마실 것도 드시겠어요?
A: 네, 레모네이드 한 잔 마시죠.
C: 같은 걸로 한 잔 더 주세요.

5. A: 실례합니다. 주문하신 것 왔습니다.
B: 고마워요.
A: 다른 것 좀 드시겠습니까?
B: 커피 좀 더 먹겠습니다.
A: 알겠습니다. 맛있게 드십시오.
……
A: 음식 어떠셨어요?
B: 맛있었어요.
A: 후식을 드시겠습니까?
B: 아니오, 배가 불러요.

C. Important Points

1.
- Do you have any specials?: (오늘) 특별 요리가 있나요?
- What comes with that?: 어떤 요리가 함께 나오죠?

2.
- circulation: 혈액 순환
- Duty Free shop: 면세점

〈건강에 관한 표현들〉

- My grandfather is always in the pink. He still goes mountain-climbing.
  내 할아버지께서는 언제나 원기왕성하시다. 아직도 등산을 다니시고 계신다.
- My mother was quite sick last summer but she's as fit as a fiddle now.
  우리 어머니께서는 지난 여름에 몹시 편찮으셨는데, 지금은 아주 건강하시다.
- as fit as a fiddle: 건강하여, 원기 왕성하여
- I exercise every morning in order to keep in condition.
  나는 건강을 유지하기 위해 매일 아침 운동을 한다.
- Now the pain is gone and I feel like a million bucks.
  이제는 통증이 가셔 기분이 아주 좋다.
- buck: (미 구어) 남자, 멋쟁이
- You are well-built.
  몸이 건강하시군요.

3.
- recipe: 요리법
- skillet: 프라이팬, 스튜냄비
- grate: 비비다, 문지르다, 뭉개다
- It'll be ready in 10 minutes.: 10분 후면 될 거야.
- My mouth is watering.: 군침이 돈다.

4.
- chowder: 생선 혹은 조개에 절인 돼지고기, 양파 등을 섞어 끓인 것.
- french fries: 감자를 채 썰어서 튀긴 것.

5.
- dessert: 후식
- Would you like anything else?: 다른 것 좀 드시겠습니까?
- Enjoy your meal.: (음식) 맛있게 드십시오.
- I'm full.: 배가 불러요.

D. Filling in the Blanks

1. A: May I take your order?
   B: Do you have _______________?
   A: Yes, today's special is linguini with clams.
   B: And ______________________________?
   A: Well, you have a choice of soup or salad.
   B: Okay. I'll have the special with a soup, please.
   A: ___________________________ would you like on your salad?
   B: I'll have the French dressing.

2. A: Excuse me, _____________________________ now.
   B: All right sir, what would you like?
   A: I'll start with a large bowl of clam chowder. And then, the seafood platter with French fries.
   B: And ma'am?
   C: I'll have the same.
   B: Would you like _____________________ with that?
   A: Yes, a glass of lemonade.
   C: ___________________________, please.

3. A: Excuse me. This is your order.
   B: Thank you.
   A: Would you like anything else?
   B: ______________________________, please.
   A: Sure. Enjoy your meal.
   ……
   A: ___________________________?
   B: It was good.
   A: Would you like some dessert?
   B: No, ___________________.

E. Dictation

1. ______________________________

2. ______________________________

3. ______________________________

4. ______________________________

5. ______________________________

6. ______________________________

7. ______________________________

8. ______________________________

9. ______________________________

10. ______________________________

11. ______________________________

12. ______________________________

13. ______________________________

14. ______________________________

15. ______________________________

3-3 공항 및 기내에서

A. Dialogue

- Listen to the teacher.
- Repeat after the teacher.
- Practice by yourself.
- Memorize the dialogue.

1. A: Excuse me, does this plane go directly to Melbourne?
   B: No, sir. You have to change planes in Sydney.
   A: What flight do I take from Sydney?
   B: The routing should be indicated on your ticket with the flight number, sir.
   A: Oh, yes, that's right. By the way, do I have to pick up my baggage in Sydney and check it through to Melbourne?
   B: No, sir. Your baggage will be checked through for you. You don't have to worry about that. You can just pick it up after you arrive in Melbourne.

2. A: Pardon me, what flight did they just call?
   B: Well, they called several. Did you have any specific one in mind?
   A: Yeah, I'm waiting for Korean Air flight 308.
   B: I don't believe that one was called, sir.
   A: Gosh, I could have sworn they did, could you please check?
   B: Certainly, sir. Wait a minute, please.

B. Practice

- Read through the dialogue in Korean.
- Repeat the dialogue in English.

1. A: 실례합니다. 이 비행기는 멜번까지 논스톱으로 운행합니까?
B: 아닙니다. 시드니에서 갈아타셔야 합니다.
A: 시드니에서 몇 편을 디지요?
B: 노선과 편명은 티켓에 기재되어 있습니다.
A: 아, 그렇군요. 그런데 제 짐은 시드니에서 찾아서 다시 멜번으로 부쳐야 하나요?
B: 아니오. 짐은 최종 목적지까지 죽 운송될 겁니다. 그 점은 염려 안 하셔 도 됩니다. 멜번에 도착한 뒤에 찾으시면 돼요.

2. A: 실례합니다. 금방 몇 호기편을 불렀습니까?
B: 여러 편을 불렀는데요, 특별히 기다리는 비행편이 있습니까?
A: 저는 대한항공 308호기편을 기다리는 중입니다.
B: 그 비행기편은 부르지 않은 것 같은데요.
A: 이런, 틀림없이 방송을 한 것 같은데, 확인 좀 해주시겠습니까?
B: 예, 잠깐만 기다리세요.

3. A: Welcome aboard, sir. May I see your boarding pass, please?
B: My what? I'm sorry, I don't understand.
A: Your boarding pass, sir. Perhaps you've got it together with your ticket.
B: Oh! you mean this? I'm sorry. Here it is.
A: Thank you. Please step to your right. Your seat is on the next aisle.
B: Thank you.

4. A: What would you like to drink, sir?
B: Well, let's see. What do you have?
A: Beer, Scotch, coke. You name it.
B: Well, I think I'll settle for a Scotch.
A: Would you like that on the rocks sir?
B: I'd prefer it with soda, if you have it.

5. A: Please fasten your seat belt, sir.
B: I really need to go to the bathroom.
A: I'm sorry, but you must wait until the seat belt light goes off.
B: Okay. But may I change my seat? It would be really nice if you could arrange it.
A: Is there a problem with this seat, sir?
B: No, I am claustrophobic and sitting in the middle isn't helping any.
A: Let me check whether there is another available seat.
B: Thanks, it's very kind of you.

3. A: 어서 오십시오. 탑승권 좀 보여주시겠습니까?
B: 뭐라고요? 죄송하지만 무슨 말씀인지 모르겠는데요.
A: 탑승권이요. 아마 항공권하고 같이 갖고 계실 거예요.
B: 아! 이것 말씀이세요? 미안합니다. 여기 있어요.
A: 감사합니다. 오른쪽으로 가십시오. 손님 좌석은 다음 통로 측에 있습니다.
B: 고맙습니다.

4. A: 어떤 걸 드시겠어요, 손님?
B: 잠깐만요. 어떤 것들이 있습니까?
A: 맥주, 위스키, 콜라가 있습니다. 말씀만 하십시오.
B: 저는 스카치로 하겠습니다.
A: 얼음을 넣어서 드시겠습니까?
B: 소다수가 있으면 그것을 넣어주셨으면 좋겠습니다.

5. A: 좌석 벨트를 매 주세요, 손님.
B: 화장실에 꼭 가야하는데요.
A: 죄송합니다만 좌석 벨트 등이 꺼질 때까지 기다리셔야만 합니다.
B: 좋습니다. 그런데 자리 좀 바꿀 수 있을까요? 그렇게 해 주시면 정말 좋겠는데요.
A: 이 자리에 무슨 문제가 있나요, 손님?
B: 아니오. 내가 밀실 공포증이 있어서 가운데 앉는 게 전혀 좋지가 않아요.
A: 다른 가용한 좌석이 있는지 알아볼게요.
B: 고맙습니다, 정말로 친절하시군요.

C. Important Points

1. • The routing should be indicted on your ticket with the flight number, sir.
노선이 편명과 함께 티켓에 표시되어 있을 겁니다.
• route: (사람, 여행을 위한) 노선을 정하다, 여행경로[코스]를 정하다

2. 〈탑승수속 방송관련 문장〉
• Pardon me, what flight did they just call?
죄송하지만, 방금 몇 호기편을 불렀습니까?
• What flight did they just announce?
방금 방송에서 몇 호기라고 했습니까?
• I couldn't quite catch the last announcement. What did they say?
안내방송의 마지막 부분을 잘 못 알아들었는데 뭐라고 했습니까?
• Did I hear that flight 358 has been delayed?
358호기가 지연된다고 그랬습니까?
• Flight 257 is now ready for boarding. All passengers for flight 257, please proceed to gate 34.
257호기가 지금 곧 탑승을 시작하겠습니다. 257호기에 타실 승객 여러분은 34번 탑승구로 나가 주십시오.
• Oh, look at the board. Boarding has started.
오, 저기 안내판 좀 보세요. 탑승을 이미 시작했군요.

3. • Please step to your right. Your seat is on the next aisle.
우측으로 들어가세요. 선생님의 좌석은 바로 다음 통로측에 있습니다.
• aisle seat: 통로측 좌석
• window seat: 창측 좌석

〈좌석을 알려 주는 표현〉

- Your seat is to the extreme left[right].
  댁의 좌석은 제일 좌측[우측]에 있습니다.
- Your seat is the second one on the left.
  댁의 좌석은 우측 제일 2번째 것입니다.
- Your seat is the last one on the right.
  댁의 좌석은 우측 제일 뒤의 것입니다.
- Your seat is in the next compartment.
  댁의 좌석은 다음 객실에 있습니다.

4. 〈기내에서 음식 관련 표현〉

- What have you got (to offer)?: 어떤 것이 있습니까?
- What's available?: 어떤 것이 가능합니까?
- What do you have for dinner tonight?
  저녁식사로 어떤 음식이 나옵니까?
- What time do you serve dinner?: 저녁은 몇 시에 나옵니까?
- You wouldn't happen to have Cognac by any chance, would you?
  혹시 꼬냑 좀 없을까요?
- I'd like it straight, please.: 아무것도 타지 말고 주시면 좋겠습니다.
- I think I'll just have some Scotch on the rocks.
  저는 위스키에 얼음을 넣어 들겠습니다.
- Scotch on the rocks, please.: 스카치위스키에 얼음을 넣어 주십시오.

5.

- Please fasten your seat belt, sir.: 좌석 벨트를 매 주세요, 손님.
- claustrophobic: 밀실 공포증의, 밀실 공포증 환자
- It's very kind of you.: 정말로 친절하시군요.

D. Filling in the Blanks

1. A: Pardon me, what flight did they just call?

   B: Well, they called several. Did you have ______________________?

   A: Yeah, I'm waiting for Korean Air flight 308.

   B: I don't believe ______________________, sir.

   A: Gosh, I could have sworn they did, ______________________?

   B: Certainly, sir. Wait a minute, please.

2. A: Welcome aboard, sir. ______________________, please?

   B: My what? I'm sorry, I don't understand.

   A: Your boarding pass, sir. Perhaps ____________ together with your ticket.

   B: Oh! you mean this? I'm sorry. Here it is.

   A: Thank you. ______________________. Your seat is on the next aisle.

   B: Thank you.

3. A: ______________________, sir.

   B: I really need to go to the bathroom.

   A: I'm sorry, but __________________ until the seat belt light goes off.

   B: Okay. But may I change my seat? It would be really nice if you could arrange it.

   A: ______________________ with this seat, sir?

   B: No, I am claustrophobic and sitting in the middle isn't helping any.

   A: Let me check whether there is another available seat.

   B: Thanks, it's very kind of you.

E. Dictation

1. ______________________________

2. ______________________________

3. ______________________________

4. ______________________________

5. ______________________________

6. ______________________________

7. ______________________________

8. ______________________________

9. ______________________________

10. ______________________________

11. ______________________________

12. ______________________________

13. ______________________________

14. ______________________________

15. ______________________________

3-4 명소 소개

A. Dialogue

- Listen to the teacher.
- Repeat after the teacher.
- Practice by yourself.
- Memorize the dialogue.

1. A: We are entering Kyoungbokgung Palace. Let's stop for a few minutes so I can explain about the palace.

B: What a wonderful palace it is! It doesn't look very old, does it?

A: No, it doesn't. But it has a long history. It was originally built in 1394, two years after the opening of the Chosun Dynasty, almost a hundred years before Columbus discovered America. As you know, we had an unlucky history in the 16th century. Hideyoshi in Japan was strong and ambitious enough to invade the Korean Peninsula. His stupid ambition brought the complete destruction of this palace in 1592.

B: Did it remain in ruins for several centuries? When were the buildings rebuilt in this palace?

A: Yes, it did. But the buildings were built again in the reign of King Kojong by his father, who was his regent at the time. Come this way, please…. We are standing in front of Keunjeongjeon Hall.

B: What a gorgeous building!

B. Practice

- Read through the dialogue in Korean.
- Repeat the dialogue in English.

1. A: 우리는 경복궁에 들어서고 있어요. 몇분간만 멈추었다 가시죠. 그 동안에 이 궁궐에 대해서 설명하겠습니다.

B: 정말 아름다운 궁궐이군요! 그렇게 오래돼 보이지는 않는군요, 그렇죠?

A: 네, 그렇게 오래돼 보이지 않지요. 하지만 이것은 긴 역사를 가지고 있답니다. 이것은 원래 1394년에 중건되었는데 조선 왕조가 문을 연지 바로 2년 후였죠. 그리고 이것은 콜럼버스가 미국을 발견하기 거의 100년 전이었죠. 아시겠지만 우리는 16세기에 불행한 역사가 있었어요. 일본의 히데요시는 강하고 한반도를 침략할 만큼 야망이 있었어요. 그의 어리석은 야망이 이 궁궐을 1592년에 완전히 파괴시켰습니다.

B: 수세기동안 그것은 황폐화된 채로 남아있었나요? 이 궁궐안의 건물들은 언제 재건되었나요?

A: 네, 그래요. 하지만 이 건물들은 고종 시대에 당시 섭정이었던 그의 아버지에 의해서 다시 지어졌어요. 이리로 와 보세요. 우리는 근정전 앞에서 있어요.

B: 정말 아름다운 건물이군요!

2. A: Would you like to take a scenic tour today?

B: Yes, I'd like to go someplace not far from the city.

A: Let's go to Kanghwado Island. It has a long history and it's not far from here.

B: Sure, whatever you recommend.

A: Let's start at Kapkot Fort. It's usually the first place tourists reach after landing on the island.

B: Oh, look! What were those devices used for?

A: They're guns used during the late Chosun Dynasty. This fort was the site of a battle. Korean soldiers exchanged fierce cannon fire with foreign warships. The two guns are still installed there.

B: I see.

2. A: 오늘 경치 좋은 곳으로 관광하시겠습니까?

B: 네, 시에서 멀지 않은 곳으로 가고 싶어요.

A: 강화도로 가시죠. 그 섬은 긴 역사를 가지고 있고 여기서부터 그렇게 멀지 않죠.

B: 좋습니다. 당신이 추천하는 곳이라면 어디든지 가죠.

A: 갑곶 성채에서 시작하시죠. 그곳은 관광객들이 섬에 도착한 후 대개 맨 먼저 찾는 장소죠.

B: 아, 보세요! 저 장치들은 무엇에 사용된 것이죠?

A: 그것들은 조선 왕조 후기 시대에 사용된 포들이었죠. 이 성채는 전투 장소였지요. 조선 병사들은 외국 군함들과 격렬한 포격전을 전개했죠. 두 대의 대포가 여전히 거기에 설치되어 있죠.

B: 이, 알겠어요.

C. Important Points

1.
- in the reign of: -의 왕대에, -의 치세에
- regent: 섭정(攝政)
- for the time being: 당분간, 우선은

2.
- fort: 성채, 요새, 보루
- gun: 대포, 포, 총
- cannon: 대포
- warship: 군함, 전함
- Whatever you recommend.: 당신이 추천하는 곳이라면 어디든지 (가죠).

D. Filling in the Blanks

1. A: We are entering Kyoungbokgung Palace. Let's stop for a few minutes so ______________________________.

B: What a wonderful palace it is! ______________________, does it?

A: No, it doesn't. But it has a long history. It was originally built in 1394, ______________ the opening of the Chosun Dynasty, almost a hundred years before Columbus discovered America. As you know, we had an unlucky history in the 16th century. Hideyoshi in Japan was strong and ambitious ______________ the Korean Peninsula. His stupid ambition brought the complete destruction of this palace in 1592.

B: Did it ______________ for several centuries? When were the buildings rebuilt in this palace?

A: Yes, it did. But the buildings were built again in the reign of King Kojong by his father, who was his regent at the time. Come this way, please…. We are standing in front of Keunjeongjeon Hall.

B: __________________________!

2. A: Would you like to take a scenic tour today?

B: Yes, I'd like to go ______________________________.

A: Let's go to Kanghwado Island. ____________________ and it's not far from here.

B: Sure, whatever you recommend.

A: Let's start at Kapkot Fort. It's usually ____________ tourists reach after landing on the island.

B: Oh, look! What were ______________________?

A: They're guns used during the late Chosun Dynasty. This fort was the site of a battle. ________________________ fierce cannon fire with foreign warships. The two guns are still installed there.

B: I see.

E. Dictation

1. ______________________________

2. ______________________________

3. ______________________________

4. ______________________________

5. ______________________________

6. ______________________________

7. ______________________________

8. ______________________________

9. ______________________________

10. ______________________________

11. ______________________________

12. ______________________________

13. ______________________________

14. ______________________________

15. ______________________________

PART 2

무역영어회화편

PART 2

1. 설명과 협상

1-1 제품 설명

A. Dialogue

- Listen to the teacher.
- Repeat after the teacher.
- Practice by yourself.
- Memorize the dialogue.

1. A: I strongly recommend these products.
   B: What are their strong points?
   A: There are lots of things to be said about them. In the first place they are more durable than any similar products on the market.
   B: Why does it wear longer than the others?
   A: The yarn is carefully selected for quality and woven very tightly in this fabric.
   B: Do you have any test results on that?

2. A: Mr. Clark, our model can't be compared with others.
   B: Well, in what ways, for example?
   A: It's lighter in weight, for one, which makes it easier to carry around.
   B: Well, that's a point in your favor.
   A: In addition, it's lower in price. What else could you ask for?
   B: How about its adaptability? Can it be used on both AC-DC current?

Business English Conversation

B. Practice

- Read through the dialogue in Korean.
- Repeat the dialogue in English.

1. A: 이 제품들을 강력히 추천합니다.

   B: 강점이 무엇이죠?

   A: 말씀 드릴 것들이 많습니다. 우선 시장에 나와 있는 유사한 제품들보다 더 내구성이 있습니다.

   B: 왜 다른 것들보다 더 오래 입을 수 있죠?

   A: 이 천은 질을 높이기 위해 직물실이 주의깊게 선택되었고 매우 촘촘하게 짜기 때문입니다.

   B: 그것에 대한 시험 결과 같은 것이 있습니까?

2. A: 클락씨, 저희 모델은 타사 모델과 비교가 안됩니다.

   B: 예를 들면 어떤 측면에서요?

   A: 무게가 우선 더 가볍고요, 그래서 갖고 다니기가 더욱 용이하지요.

   B: 그것은 귀사의 제품이 갖는 유리한 점이지요.

   A: 게다가 가격도 저렴하구요. 어떤 측면을 더 물어보고 싶으세요?

   B: 적응성은 어떤가요? 즉 교류, 직류 양쪽으로 쓸 수 있나요?

3. A: Mr. Park, how would you compare your electric fans to those of other manufacturers?

B: Well, compared with other products, ours is easier to operate.

A: Well, in what ways, for example?

B: To begin with, it's fully automated. All you do is push this button and it starts.

A: Oh, yeah? And how do you stop it?

B: Just set the timer at the start, and it goes off automatically.

4. A: This is our new product.

B: What gives it the edge over its competitors?

A: The major advantage is its strength.

B: How strong is it?

A: It's about twice as strong as the usual one.

B: Hmm, I think the quality is good.

5. A: Mr. Lee, I'd like to show you our latest PC model. It works like a charm.

B: How does it go on pricing?

A: It's the most reasonably priced model on the market.

B: Have you got anything in print on it?

A: Of course. Just a minute. I'll get you some brochures on these machines.

3. A: 박 선생님, 귀사 선풍기는 타사 선풍기와 비교했을 때 어떻습니까?
B: 저, 타사 제품과 비교하여 저희 제품은 작동시키기가 더 쉽습니다.
A: 예를 들어 어떤 면에서요?
B: 우선, 완전 자동식입니다. 이 버튼만 누르시면 선풍기가 켜집니다.
A: 그래요? 그러면 끌 때는 어떻게 하지요?
B: 타이머를 시작부분에 놓으면 자동적으로 꺼집니다.

4. A: 이건 우리 신제품입니다.
B: 경쟁 제품보다 우세한 점이 무엇입니까?
A: 주된 장점은 강도에 있습니다.
B: 얼마나 강한가요?
A: 일반적인 제품보다 약 두 배 정도 강합니다.
B: 음, 품질이 우수하군요.

5. A: 이 선생님, 우리 회사의 최신 PC 모델을 보여 드리겠습니다. 신통하게 잘 작동이 됩니다.
B: 가격은 어떻게 되죠?
A: 시중에 나온 것 중 가장 저렴한 모델입니다.
B: 그것에 대해서 설명한 인쇄물이 있습니까?
A: 물론이지요, 잠깐만 기다리세요. 이 기계에 대한 인쇄물을 좀 갖다 드리겠습니다.

C. Important Points

1.
- durable: 오래 견디는, 튼튼한
- wear: 입다, 사용에 견디다, 쓸 수 있다, 오래가다
- yarn: 직물을 짜는 실, 뜨개실
- weave (wove-woven): 짜다, 짜 맞추다, 뜨다
- fabric: 피륙, 직물, 천, 구조, 조직

2.
- That's one of your strong points.
  그것은 귀사의 제품이 갖는 강점 중에 하나입니다.
- That's your item's good point. 그것은 귀사 제품의 장점입니다.
- That's to your advantage. 그것은 귀사에게 유리한 점이지요.
- to one's advantage: -에게 유리하게[한], -에게 안성맞춤으로
- That's a feather in your cap[hat]. 그것은 귀사의 자랑거리죠.
- a feather in one's cap[hat]: 훌륭한 업적 ; 자랑[영광]이 되는 것
- That's a weak point in your item. 그것은 귀사 제품의 약점입니다.
- That's your item's disadvantage.
  그것은 귀사 제품이 갖는 불리한 점입니다.
- adaptability: 적응성, 순응성, 융통성
- current: 흐름, 전류, 경향

3.
- Compared with other products, ours is easier to operate.
  타사 제품과 비교해 볼 때 저희제품은 작동시키기가 더 쉽습니다.
- To begin with, it's fully automated. 우선 완전 자동식입니다.
- 우선: to start with, for openers, to begin with, first of all
- It's completely[100%] automatic. 그것은 완전 자동입니다.
- It runs[works] by itself. 그것은 자동입니다.

4. • What gives it the edge over its competitors?
경쟁 제품보다 우세한 점이 무엇입니까?
• edge: 우세, 우세한 점
• It's about twice as strong as the usual one.
일반적인 제품보다 약 두배 정도 강합니다.

5. • It works like a charm: 신통하게 잘 작동이 됩니다.
• like a charm: 신통하게, 신기하게
• How does it go on pricing?: 가격은 어떻게 되죠?
• It's the most reasonably priced model on the market.
시중에 나온 것 중 가장 저렴한 모델입니다.

D. Filling in the Blanks

1. A: ______________________ these products.

   B: What are their strong points?

   A: There are lots of things to be said about them. ______________ they are more durable than any similar products on the market.

   B: Why does it wear ____________________?

   A: The yarn is carefully selected for quality and woven very tightly in this fabric.

   B: Do you have any test results on that?

2. A: Mr. Clark, our model can't be compared with others.

   B: Well, ______________, for example?

   A: It's lighter in weight, for one, which makes it easier ___________.

   B: Well, that's a point in your favor.

   A: In addition, it's lower in price. What else could you ask for?

   B: ____________________? Can it be used on both AC-DC current?

3. A: This is our new product.

   B: What gives it ______________________?

   A: The major advantage is its strength.

   B: ______________?

   A: It's about ____________________ the usual one.

   B: Hmm, I think the quality is good.

E. Dictation

1. ______________________________

2. ______________________________

3. ______________________________

4. ______________________________

5. ______________________________

6. ______________________________

7. ______________________________

8. ______________________________

9. ______________________________

10. ______________________________

11. ______________________________

12. ______________________________

13. ______________________________

14. ______________________________

15. ______________________________

1-2 가격 협상 및 계약

A. Dialogue

- Listen to the teacher.
- Repeat after the teacher.
- Practice by yourself.
- Memorize the dialogue.

1. A: Is this your best price?

B: I'm afraid it is. $15.70 CIF Chicago is our rock-bottom price.

A: That may be true, but if you make it cheaper, we'll place larger order with you next time.

B: About what price would you say?

A: I'd like to ask you for $15.

B: $15 is out of the question. The best price I can offer you is $15.60.

2. A: The prices you quoted are a little too expensive. I want 10% off the total.

B: I can't give you a reduction like that!

A: Hmm, I think you can manage that. I've already had a similar offer from several of your competitors.

B: However when it comes down to quality, there won't be any comparison.

A: You'd better meet my figure, if your company really wants to sell more.

B: Well, I need some time to think it over.

B. Practice

- Read through the dialogue in Korean.
- Repeat the dialogue in English.

1. A: 이게 최저가입니까?

   B: 그렇습니다. 시카고 도착 운임, 보험료 포함가격으로 15달러 70센트가 우리가 해드릴 수 있는 최저가입니다.

   A: 그러시겠지만 더 싸게 주시면 다음에 더 많이 주문하겠습니다.

   B: 얼마를 말씀하시는 거죠?

   A: 15달러로 해주십사고 부탁드립니다.

   B: 15달러는 말도 안됩니다. 제가 드릴 수 있는 가장 최저 가격은 15달러 60센트입니다.

2. A: 견적하신 가격이 좀 비싸군요.
   총액에서 10%를 낮춰 주셨으면 하는데요.

   B: 그만큼 낮춰 드릴 수는 없습니다!

   A: 음, 제가 제시한 가격이 가능하실 텐데요. 귀사 경쟁업체 몇 군데로부터 이미 유사한 제안을 받았는데요.

   B: 그렇지만 품질을 생각하신다면 비교할 대상이 없을텐데요.

   A: 귀사가 물건을 정말로 더 파시길 원한다면 제가 제시한 가격을 맞추시는 것이 좋을 겁니다.

   B: 음, 생각할 시간이 더 필요합니다.

3. A: How much does it cost per unit?
B: Our factory price is $3.30 per unit. But it depends on quantity.
A: Suppose I order 20,000….
B: Then, I can bring it down to $3.25.
A: That doesn't seem like much of a reduction. How about $3.20?
B: If you double the order, I can meet your price.

4. A: Mr. Hong, we've looked over the agreement, but we have some questions. The first is in regard to terms.
B: Oh, I thought it said two years.
A: It does, but our question is in regard to renewal.
B: The agreement will be renewed annually.
A: Do you agree to that?
B: Yes, we have no objection to renewing the contract for another year upon consent of both parties.

5. A: Okay, Mr. Watson. The contract's all drawn up and ready to sign.
B: Fine, let's have a look at it.
A: I'm sure you'll find everything in order.
B: Wait. Hold on a second. You left out the point about the delivery date.
A: Did I really? I could have sworn it was included along with the other items.
B: Well, here. Take a look for yourself.

3. A: 개당 가격이 얼마입니까?
B: 공장도 가격은 개당 3달러 30센트입니다. 하지만 그것은 수량에 따라 결정됩니다.
A: 20,000개를 주문할까 생각하고 있습니다만….
B: 그렇다면 3달러 25센트로 깎아 드릴 수 있습니다.
A: 많이 깎아 주는 것도 아니네요. 3달러 20센트는 어때요?
B: 두 배를 주문하시면 제시하신 가격에 맞추어 드릴 수 있습니다.

4. A: 홍 선생님, 저희가 계약서를 검토해 봤습니다만, 몇 가지 의문점이 있더군요. 그 첫번째가 계약기간에 관한 것입니다.
B: 계약서에 2년으로 되어 있는 줄로 알고 있는데요.
A: 맞습니다. 하지만 저희가 알고 싶은 건 갱신에 관한 것입니다.
B: 계약은 매년마다 갱신될 것입니다.
A: 거기에 동의하세요?
B: 예, 저희도 쌍방의 합의에 의해 계약을 1년 더 연장하는 것에 동의합니다.

5. A: 왓슨씨, 계약서는 다 작성되었으니까 이제 서명만 하시면 됩니다.
B: 그래요? 어디 한번 봅시다.
A: 모든 게 다 제대로 되어 있을 겁니다.
B ; 잠깐만요. 인도일에 관한 부분을 빠뜨리셨는데요.
A: 정말요? 분명히 다른 항목들과 함께 기재되어 있을 텐데요.
B: 저, 여기요. 직접 한번 보세요.

C. Important Points

1.
- Is this your best price?: 이게 최저가입니까?
- CIF: 운임, 보험료 포함가격 (Cost, insurance and freight)
- rock-bottom price: 최저 가격, 최하 가격

2.
- quote: 견적하다, 시가를 말하다
- I want 10% off the total.: 총액에서 10%를 낮춰 주셨으면 하는데요.
- when it comes (down) to: ~에 관해서는
- When it comes down to quality, there won't be any comparison.
  품질에 대해서는 비교할 대상이 없을 텐데요.
- meet: 맞추다, 만족시키다, 응하다
- think over: 재고하다, 숙고하다

3.
- bring down: 물가를 떨어뜨리다, 가격을 내리다
- suppose: -라고 가정하다

4.
- agreement: 계약(서)
- in regard to: -에 관한, -에 관해서
- The contract will be up for renewal every year.
  그 계약은 매년 갱신될 것입니다.
- be up for: (진급 · 재판 · 시험 등의)대상으로 오르다.
- The contract calls for an annual renewal.
  그 계약은 매년 갱신을 필요로 합니다.
- call for: -을 요구하다, -을 필요로 하다

5. • Hold on a second. You left out the part about the delivery date.
잠깐만요, 인도일에 관한 부분을 빠뜨리셨네요.

• leave out: 생략하다, 제외하다

• You omitted[missed]the delivery date. 인도일을 빠뜨리셨군요.

• Oh, you forgot the part about the delivery date.
이런, 인도일에 관한 사 항을 잊으셨군요.

• I can't find anything about the delivery date.
인도일에 관한 사항이 보이지 않네요.

• I'm sure you'll find everything in order.
모든 게 다 제대로 되어 있을 겁니다.

D. Filling in the Blanks

1. A: ______________________________ per unit?

   B: Our factory price is $3.30 per unit. But ______________________________.

   A: Suppose I order 20,000….

   B: Then, I can bring it down to $3.25.

   A: That doesn't seem like ______________________. How about $3.20?

   B: If you double the order, I can meet your price.

2. A: Mr. Hong, we've looked over the agreement, but we have some questions. The first is ______________________.

   B: Oh, I thought it said two years.

   A: It does, but our question is in regard to renewal.

   B: The agreement ______________________________.

   A: Do you agree to that?

   B: Yes, ______________________ to renewing the contract for another year upon consent of both parties.

3. A: Okay, Mr. Watson. The contract's ________________ and ready to sign.

   B: Fine, let's have a look at it.

   A: I'm sure you'll find everything in order.

   B: Wait. Hold on a second. You __________________ about the delivery date.

   A: Did I really? I could have sworn it was included along with the other items.

   B: Well, here. ______________________________.

E. Dictation

1. ______________________________

2. ______________________________

3. ______________________________

4. ______________________________

5. ______________________________

6. ______________________________

7. ______________________________

8. ______________________________

9. ______________________________

10. ______________________________

11. ______________________________

12. ______________________________

13. ______________________________

14. ______________________________

15. ______________________________

PART 2

2. 조건과 주문

2-1 조건 설명

A. Dialogue

- Listen to the teacher.
- Repeat after the teacher.
- Practice by yourself.
- Memorize the dialogue.

1. A: How soon can you make the delivery?
   B: Within eight weeks.
   A: We can't lose the season. Please deliver four weeks earlier.
   B: Four weeks? That's pretty tight.
   A: However it's really important for us.
   B: All right. I'll see if I can make it.

2. A: Mr. Baker, we'd like to place an order for 300 units of model A23 with you.
   B: Thank you. What do you have in mind in the way of a delivery date?
   A: Can you make the initial delivery in May?
   B: Certainly, we can.

Business English Conversation

B. Practice

- Read through the dialogue in Korean.
- Repeat the dialogue in English.

1. A: 인도를 얼마나 빨리 해 주실 수 있습니까?
B: 8주 안에 해 드리겠습니다.
A: 제 철을 놓칠 수는 없습니다. 4주 더 빨리 인도해 주십시오.
B: 4주라고요? 그건 우리에게 너무 빡빡한데요.
A: 하지만 그건 우리에게 정말로 중요합니다.
B: 좋습니다. 그렇게 할 수 있는지 알아보겠습니다.

2. A: 베이커씨, 모델 A23 300대를 귀사에 주문하고 싶습니다.
B: 감사합니다. 인도일은 언제로 생각하고 계십니까?
A: 첫 인도를 5월 중에 해 주실 수 있습니까?
B: 물론 그렇게 해 드릴 수 있습니다.

3. A: Ms. Kim, I think you can't go wrong with this machine.
B: Well, how long is the warranty?
A: It's good for two years.
B: And after that?
A: There's a slight service charge.
B: Sounds okay to me, as long as it works well.

4. A: What about the cost of delivery?
B: We'd like to do it in accordance with an FOB contract.
A: That's FOB Incheon, right?
B: Yes, that's how we've been handling all our contracts recently.
A: What about insuring the shipment?
B: I'm afraid you'll have to take care of the insurance. That's our standard practice in this type of contract.
A: All right, let me talk it over with my staff. I'll get back to you tomorrow with an answer.
B: Fine.

5. A: What line are you planning to send the shipment on?
B: I think "KOR" line is the best. I know it's the fastest.
A: What are the ports of call? Do you happen to know?
B: I believe they are Nagoya, Singapore and Brisbane.
A: Did you book space on any vessel yet?
B: Yes, M.S. "Moogunghwa" departing Busan on March 3.

3. A: 김 선생님, 이 기계를 선택하시면 전혀 문제가 없을 겁니다.
B: 저, 보증기간은 얼마나 되나요?
A: 이년 동안입니다.
B: 그 후에는요?
A: 약간의 서비스료를 내야 합니다.
B: 괜찮을 것 같은데요. 성능만 좋다면요.

4. A: 인도운임은 어떻게 하시겠습니까?
B: 본선인도조건으로 계약했으면 합니다.
A: 본선인도조건 인천 말씀이지요?
B: 그렇습니다. 저희는 모든 계약에 대해서 최근에 바로 그렇게 거래해 왔습니다.
A: 적하(선적화물)에 대한 보험가입은 어떻게 하시겠습니까?
B: 보험가입은 귀사에서 해결하실 문제지요. 이런 종류의 계약에서는 그것이 표준관례입니다.
A: 좋습니다. 저희 간부들과 상의해 보겠습니다. 내일 다시 연락하여 답변 드리겠습니다.
B: 좋습니다.

5. A: 선적은 어떤 선박회사를 통해 하실 계획이십니까?
B: KOR 선박회사가 제일 좋다고 봅니다. 가장 빠르거든요.
A: 방문하는 항구가 어디죠? 혹시 아세요?
B: 나고야, 싱가포르, 브리즈번으로 알고 있습니다.
A: 선복은 예약해 놓았습니까?
B: 네, 3월 3일에 부산을 떠나는 "무궁화호"입니다.

C. Important Points

1. • delivery: 인도
   • We can't lose the season.: 제 철을 놓칠 수는 없습니다.
   • I'll see if I can make it.: 그렇게 할 수 있는지 알아보겠습니다.

2. • place an order: 주문하다
   • What do you have in mind in the way of a delivery date?
   인도일은 언제로 생각하고 계십니까?

3. • You can't go wrong with this machine.
   이 기계를 선택하시면 전혀 문제가 없습니다.
   • How long is the warranty?: 보증기간은 얼마나 되지요?
   • warranty: (품질 등의) 보증, 보증서
   • What's your warranty period?: 보증기간이 얼마나 됩니까?
   • How long is the warranty good for [valid]?
   품질보증은 얼마동안 유효합니까?

〈warranty 관련표현〉

• What's the warranty? 품질보증의 내용은 어떤 것입니까?
• Does this machine have any warranty? 이 기계는 품질보증을 해줍니까?
• The company didn't tell me there was no warranty when I bought this machine.
내가 이 기계를 살 때 그 회사는 품질보증이 없다는 사실을 말해주지 않았습니다.
• What kind of after-sale(s) service do you do?
어떤 애프터서비스를 해 줍니까?
• 애프터서비스: after-sale(s) service

4. - FOB: 본선 인도 (=Free on Board)
- shipment: 선적, 선하, 적하위탁화물
- I'm afraid you'll have to take care of the insurance.
(적하에 대한) 보험가입은 그쪽에서 처리하실 문제지요.
- That's our standard practice in this type of contract.
이런 계약에서는 그것이 표준관례입니다.
- take care of: 책임지다, 처리하다
- standard practice 표준관행, 표준관례 (=normal way, usual way)
- That's the way we usually do[handle] it.
우린 보통 그런 식으로 그 문제를 처리하고 있지요.
- That's our usual way of doing it.
그것은 저희가 하는 통상적인 방법입니다.

5. - line: 선박회사, 선사
- port of call: 방문하는 항구, 기항
- space: 선복 (船腹) = vessel space
- vessel: 큰 배
- M.S.: 발동기선 (=Motor Ship)

D. Filling in the Blanks

1. A: How soon ______________________?
   B: Within eight weeks.
   A: ______________________. Please deliver four weeks earlier.
   B: Four weeks? That's pretty tight.
   A: However it's really important for us.
   B: All right. I'll see ______________________.

2. A: Mr. Baker, we'd like to ____________ for 300 units of model A23 with you.
   B: Thank you. ______________________ in the way of a delivery date?
   A: Can you make ________________ in May?
   B: Certainly, we can.

3. A: Ms. Kim, I think ______________________ with this machine.
   B: Well, how long is the warranty?
   A: It's good ________________.
   B: And after that?
   A: There's a slight service charge.
   B: Sounds okay to me, __________________________.

E. Dictation

1.

2.

3.

4.

5.

6.

7.

8.

9.

10.

11.

12.

13.

14.

15.

2-2 주문 및 계약

A. Dialogue

- Listen to the teacher.
- Repeat after the teacher.
- Practice by yourself.
- Memorize the dialogue.

1. A: Ms. Tailor, I'm sold on that sample. This is the sweater I have in mind. I need 36,000 units. Can you fill this order?
   B: No problem. What size and color do you have in mind?
   A: Large, medium and small in blue and green.

2. A: We pride ourselves on quality, that's our best selling point.
   B: The only problem is price. We have to ask you for a 15 percent reduction.
   A: If so, can't you increase the quantity?
   B: You don't have to worry. We've expanded our sales network. We are ready to double our order.
   A: Then I think we could reduce it by 15 percent.
   B: Thanks. Let's make the contract now.

3. A: Well, I guess that does it, Mr. Park. Where do I sign?
   B: Please put your signature here.
   A: Oh, damn it. This pen is not working.
   B: Here is my pen.
   A: Oh, thanks. How many copies do I have to sign?
   B: Two. One for each of us.

B. Practice

- Read through the dialogue in Korean.
- Repeat the dialogue in English.

1. A: 테일러씨, 저 견본품이 마음에 듭니다. 이것이 제 마음에 드는 스웨터입니다. 36,000벌이 필요합니다. 이 주문에 맞춰 주실 수 있습니까?
   B: 물론입니다. 크기와 색상은 어떻게 할까요?
   A: 대, 중, 소 크기에 청색과 녹색으로 주세요.

2. A: 우리는 품질을 자랑으로 여기고 있습니다. 그것이 우리의 최대의 판매 강점입니다.
   B: 유일한 문제는 가격입니다. 15퍼센트를 깎아 주셔야겠습니다.
   A: 그렇다면 (주문) 수량을 증가시킬 수 없습니까?
   B: 걱정마십시오. 우리는 판매망을 확장했습니다. 주문을 배로 늘릴 수가 있습니다.
   A: 그렇다면 15퍼센트를 할인해 드릴 수 있습니다.
   B: 감사합니다. 지금 계약을 맺읍시다.

3. A: 저, 그러면 다 된 것 같군요, 박 선생님. 어디다 서명하면 되지요?
   B: 여기에 서명을 해주십시오.
   A: 오, 이런, 펜이 안 나오는데요.
   B: 여기 제 것을 사용하세요.
   A: 오, 감사합니다. 서명을 몇 부 해야 합니까?
   B: 2부입니다. 쌍방에 한 부씩 해서요.

4. A: Now I think we've been able to come to an agreement.
B: Yes, all the problems have been adjusted in my opinion.
A: Right. So let's put it in writing and sign it.
B: Just a second, please. May I confirm one particular point?
A: Sure, what is it?
B: Does this contract include residual payment?
A: Of course.
B: Okay, then I'll sign it with pleasure.

5. A: I think we can go ahead and make up the contract.
B: Yes. How long should the contract term be?
A: Generally, we make our contracts for a period of one year.
B: Hmm, how about making it two years.

4. A: 자, 이젠 계약을 해도 될 것 같습니다.
B: 예, 제가 보기에도 모든 문제점들이 조정된 것 같습니다.
A: 맞습니다. 그러면 문서화해서 서명을 하도록 합시다.
B: 잠깐만요, 한 가지 사항만 더 확인을 해도 될까요?
A: 물론이죠, 뭡니까?
B: 이 계약은 잔여미불금에 대한 것도 포함하고 있습니까?
A: 그럼요.
B: 좋습니다. 그럼 기꺼이 서명을 하겠습니다.

5. A: 어서 계약서를 작성하는 것이 좋겠습니다.
B: 네. 계약 기간은 얼마로 해야 하나요?
A: 보통, 우리는 1년 기간의 계약을 합니다.
B: 음, 2년으로 하면 어떨까요?

C. Important Points

1.
- be sold on: 좋다고 믿다, 찬성하다.
- I'm sold on that sample.: 저 견본품이 마음에 듭니다.
- fill: (주문을) 받다, -을 이행하다, 충족시키다.
- Can you fill this order?: 이 주문을 이행하실 수 있습니까?

2.
- That's our best selling point.: 그것이 우리의 최대 판매 강점입니다.
- Can't you increase the quantity?: 수량을 증가시킬 수 없습니까?
- We are ready to double our order.
  주문을 배로 늘릴 준비가 되어 있습니다.

3.
- Where do I sign?: 어디에 서명을 하면 되지요?
- Please put your signature here.: 여기에 서명을 해주십시오.
- Please sign over here. 여기에 서명을 해주십시오.

〈'이제 다 되었다'의 유사 표현〉

- That does it.: 이제 됐어, 그것이면 충분해
- I guess that settles it.: 그러면 해결이 된다고 생각합니다.
- I guess that's all.: 그게 전부일 겁니다.
- I guess we're done.: 이제 다 끝난 것 같습니다.
- Everything has been taken care of.: 모든 것이 다 처리된 것 같습니다.

4.
- Let's put it in writing and sign it. 그것을 문서화해서 서명을 합시다.
- Let's get it down in writing and sign it. 그것을 문서화해서 서명합시다.
- get down: 적어두다 (write, note, record)
- Let's make it legal. 법적으로 유효하게 만듭시다.
- Let's make out the contract and sign it. 계약서를 작성한 다음 서명합시다.
- make out: (문서 등을)작성하다
- contract: 계약, 계약서

5.
- go ahead and: 어서 (구어로 재촉하는 뜻)
- make up the contract: 계약서를 작성하다

D. Filling in the Blanks

1. A: Ms. Tailor, I'm sold on that sample. This is the sweater I have in mind. I need 36,000 units. ____________________________?

   B: No problem. ________________________ do you have in mind?

   A: Large, medium and small ______________________.

2. A: We _________________ on quality, that's our best selling point.

   B: The only problem is price. We have to ask you for a 15 percent reduction.

   A: If so, ______________________ the quantity?

   B: You don't have to worry. We've expanded our sales network. We are ready to double our order.

   A: Then I think _____________________ by 15 percent.

   B: Thanks. Let's make the contract now.

3. A: Well, I guess that does it, Mr. Park. _______________________?

   B: Please _______________________ here.

   A: Oh, damn it. This pen is not working.

   B: Here is my pen.

   A: Oh, thanks. _____________________ do I have to sign?

   B: Two. One for each of us.

E. Dictation

1. ______________________________

2. ______________________________

3. ______________________________

4. ______________________________

5. ______________________________

6. ______________________________

7. ______________________________

8. ______________________________

9. ______________________________

10. ______________________________

11. ______________________________

12. ______________________________

13. ______________________________

14. ______________________________

15. ______________________________

PART 2 3. 신용장과 선적

3-1 신용장

A. Dialogue

- Listen to the teacher.
- Repeat after the teacher.
- Practice by yourself.
- Memorize the dialogue.

1. A: When can you open the L/C?

B: By the 31st of July.

A: If you want an early delivery, please give us the order details and L/C as soon as possible.

B: I see.

A: What conditions will be written on the L/C?

B: Please refer to our purchase order sheet. All the things are spelled out there.

A: Who will make out the inspection certificate?

Business English Conversation

B. Practice

- Read through the dialogue in Korean.
- Repeat the dialogue in English.

1. A: 신용장은 언제 개설하실 수 있죠?

   B: 7월 31일까지 개설할 수 있습니다.

   A: 조기 인도를 원하시면 주문 명세서와 신용장을 가능한 한 속히 보내 주십시오.

   B: 알겠습니다.

   A: 신용장에는 어떤 조건들이 명시되나요?

   B: 우리 회사의 구매 주문서를 참조해 주세요. 거기에 모든 것이 자세히 설명되어 있습니다.

   A: 누가 검사 보고서를 작성합니까?

2. A: Mr. Carter, I'd like to ask you to amend your L/C No. 2753.

B: In what ways?

A: The L/C says that partial shipment is prohibited although it is allowed in the contract.

B: Hmm, I think we made a mistake when we applied for the L/C.

A: Could you please send a fax and request amendment as quickly as possible?

B: Sure, I'll do that.

3. A: When can you give me the order detail?

B: By the end of March.

A: When can you open the L/C?

B: The fifth of April.

A: If you want an early delivery, please give us the order detail and L/C as soon as possible. We don't have enough time.

B: I see.

A: What conditions will be specified on the L/C?

B: Please refer to our purchase order sheet. Everything is spelled out in detail there.

A: Then, who will make out the inspection certificate?

2. A: 카터씨, 귀사의 신용장 2753호에 대한 수정을 부탁드립니다.
B: 어떻게요?
A: 계약서에는 분할선적이 허용되어 있는데 신용장에는 그것이 금지되어 있습니다.
B: 음, 우리가 신용장 개설을 신청할 때 실수를 한 것 같습니다.
A: 팩스를 보내셔서 가능한한 빨리 수정을 요청해 주시겠습니까?
B: 물론이죠, 그렇게 하죠.

3. A: 주문명세서를 언제 보내주시겠습니까?
B: 3월말까지 보내죠.
A: 신용장은 언제 개설하실 수 있습니까?
B: 4월 5일까지 할 수 있습니다.
A: 조기인도를 원하시면 주문명세서와 신용장을 가능한 한 빨리 보내주십시오. 시간이 충분치 않거든요.
B: 알겠습니다.
A: 신용장에는 어떤 조건들이 명시되나요?
B: 저희의 구매주문서를 참조해 주십시오. 거기에 모든 것이 상세히 명시되어 있으니까요.
A: 그렇다면 검사보고서는 누가 작성합니까?

4. A: Mr. Clark, in your Fax No. 2014 dated July 23rd, you said that you had already opened an L/C covering order No. 357, but we still haven't received any notification.

B: Really? We applied for that L/C on May 15th. It should have been here by now.

A: Hmm, then let me check the advising bank. (after a while) They say that they have not received it yet. So would you do me a favor and contact your opening bank on the matter?

B: Okay, I'll do that.

A: If it doesn't arrive by this Friday, we'll face a problem in meeting your shipment date.

5. A: Mr. Choi, I'd like to place an order for 42,000 units of sweaters.

B: OK. Can you give me a little more on the exact specifications?

A: Oh, this is a repeat order of style Y-32.

B: How about the L/C? Will you open a new one?

A: Well, I think you still have three L/Cs we opened that still have some balance left on them.

B: Yeah, right. Then to which L/C should I allocate this order?

4. A: 클라크씨, 7월 23일자 귀사 팩스 2014호를 보면 귀사께서 주문 357호에 관한 신용장을 이미 개설했다고 되어 있는데, 저희는 아직 아무런 통지도 못 받았습니다.

B: 그렇습니까? 우린 5월 15일에 그 신용장의 개설신청을 했습니다. 지금쯤이면 여기 도착되어 있어야 하는데요.

A: 음, 그러면 통지은행에 알아보겠습니다. (잠시 후) 통지은행에서도 아직 받지 못했답니다. 어려운 부탁이지만 귀사의 개설은행에 연락해서 그 문제에 대해서 좀 알아봐 주시겠습니까?

B: 좋습니다, 해보겠습니다.

A: 그것이 이번 주 금요일까지 도착하지 않으면, 선적일자를 맞추는데 문제가 생길 겁니다.

5. A: 최 선생님, 스웨터 42,000벌을 주문하고 싶은데요.

B: 좋습니다. 정확한 규격에 대해 좀 더 알려주시겠습니까?

A: 아 이것은 Y-32 스타일에 대한 재주문입니다.

B: 신용장은 어떻게 할까요? 새로 개설하시겠습니까?

A: 글쎄요, 저희가 개설한 3개의 신용장을 귀사가 갖고 있으실 것이고 거기에 아직 잔액이 좀 남아있을 겁니다.

B: 예, 맞습니다. 그러면 이 주문을 어느 신용장에 적용시켜야 할까요?

C. Important Points

1.
- L/C: 신용장 (=Letter of Credit)
- purchase order sheet: 구매 주문서
- inspection certificate: 검사 보고서, 검품 보고서
- spell out: 자세히 설명하다
- All the things are spelled out there.
  거기에 모든 것이 자세히 설명되어 있습니다.

2.
- amend: 수정하다
- amendment: 수정
- apply for the L/C: 신용장 개설을 신청하다.
- partial shipment: 분할 선적

3.
- Please refer to our purchase order sheet.
  저희 구매주문서를 참조해 주세요.
- refer to: 참조하다
- Please see our purchase order sheet.
  저희 구매주문서를 참조해 주십시오.
- order detail: 주문 명세서
- early delivery: 조기 인도

4.
- It should have been here by now.: 지금쯤이면 도착했어야 하는데.
- would [should] have p.p.: …했(었)더라면 좋았다, 하고 싶었다.
- advising bank: 통지은행
- opening bank: 개설은행

5. ● To which L/C should I allocate this order?
이 주문은 어느 신용장에 적용을 시켜야 합니까?

● allocate: 배분하다, …을 배치하다 (=apply, place)

● exact specifications: 정확한 규격

● repeat order: 재주문

● balance: 차액, 차감잔액

D. Filling in the Blanks

1. A: When ______________________?

   B: By the 31st of July.

   A: If you want an early delivery, ______________________ and L/C as soon as possible.

   B: I see.

   A: What conditions will be written on the L/C?

   B: Please ______________________. All the things are spelled out there.

   A: Who will make out the inspection certificate?

2. A: Mr. Carter, ______________________ your L/C No. 2753.

   B: In what ways?

   A: The L/C says that ______________________ although it is allowed in the contract.

   B: Hmm, I think ________________ when we applied for the L/C.

   A: Could you please send a fax and request amendment as quickly as possible?

   B: Sure, I'll do that.

3. A: Mr. Choi, I'd like to ______________ for 42,000 units of sweaters.

   B: OK. Can you give me a little more on the exact specifications?

   A: Oh, ________________ of style Y-32.

   B: How about the L/C? ______________________?

   A: Well, I think you still have three L/Cs we opened that still have some balance left on them.

   B: Yeah, right. Then to which L/C should I allocate this order?

E. Dictation

1. ______

2. ______

3. ______

4. ______

5. ______

6. ______

7. ______

8. ______

9. ______

10. ______

11. ______

12. ______

13. ______

14. ______

15. ______

3-2 선적

A. Dialogue

- Listen to the teacher.
- Repeat after the teacher.
- Practice by yourself.
- Memorize the dialogue.

1. A: Mr. Jung, how soon can you make shipment?
   B: I'd say somewhere around the 10th of June.
   A: Do you know if it'll be a direct shipment?
   B: Yeah, as far as I know.
   A: Is the vessel a containerized one?
   B: Yes, I booked space on a containerized vessel.

2. A: What's the problem?
   B: we have some unexpected production delays.
   Please extend the shipping date by one week.
   A: No, we made an agreement already. You have to finish the shipment on time.
   B: But we won't be able to make it. I hope you understand we are proceeding as quickly as we can.
   A: Okay, however this should be the last time.
   If you can't supply them by then, we will be forced to cancel the contract.

B. Practice

- Read through the dialogue in Korean.
- Repeat the dialogue in English.

1. A: 정 선생님, 선적을 얼마나 빨리 해주실 수 있습니까?
   B: 6월 10일경 쯤 될 겁니다.
   A: 직항선에 의한 선적인가요?
   B: 제가 아는 한은 그렇습니다.
   A: 컨테이너선인가요?
   B: 예, 컨테이너선을 수배해 뒀습니다.

2. A: 무슨 일이죠?
   B: 예기치 못한 생산 지연이 생겨서요. 선적일을 한주만 늦춰 주세요.
   A: 안됩니다. 우린 이미 계약을 맺었습니다. 선적을 제 때에 끝내셔야 합니다.
   B: 하지만 그렇게 할 수가 없습니다. 가능한한 빨리 진척시키고 있다는 것을 이해해 주시기를 바랍니다.
   A: 좋습니다. 하지만 이번이 마지막이어야 합니다. 그 때까지 공급하지 못하면 계약을 취소하지 않을 수 없습니다.

3. A: How long do you think the shipment will take?

B: If my guess is correct, about three months or so.

A: Really? Why is it so long?

B: There are very few direct sailings.

A: That is a problem then, isn't it?

B: Yeah, but they say there will be more frequent service starting in two months time.

4. A: When can you ship our order No. 357 of 300 men's jumpers?

B: This week.

A: Okay, did you book space on any vessel yet?

B: Yes, on Amland Line "American Voyager" departing Busan, November 11th.

A: Does it go direct or via Yokohama?

B: Direct. It arrives in Seattle on November 30th.

5. A: We found that the last shipment was short by three boxes.

B: Really? We are very sorry if it's true. I'll just check. (after a while) You are right.

A: Three boxes against the document, which specifies twenty.

B: How can I compensate you for loss?

A: Why don't you make out the invoice with a reduction of $360 next time?

3. A: 선적품이 도착하는데 얼마나 오래 걸릴까요?

B: 제 짐작이 맞다면, 약 3개월쯤 걸릴 겁니다.

A: 정말요? 왜 그렇게 오래 걸리죠?

B: 직항선이 거의 없다시피 합니다.

A: 그렇다면 문제가 되겠군요.

B: 그래요. 하지만 두 달 후부터는 더 자주 운항한다고 하더군요.

4. A: 우리의 주문번호 357, 남성용 잠바 300벌이 언제 선적됩니까?

B: 이번 주에 됩니다.

A: 좋습니다. 선복은 수배해 놓았습니까?

B: 예, Amland사의 11월 11일 부산발 'Amercian Voyager'호입니다.

A: 직항선 입니까, 요코하마 경유선 입니까?

B: 직항선 입니다. 11월 30일에 시애틀 도착입니다.

5. A: 지난 선적분에서 3상자가 부족한 것을 발견했습니다.

B: 정말입니까? 그것이 사실이라면 정말 죄송합니다. 확인 좀 해보겠습니다. (잠시 후) 선생님 말이 맞습니다.

A: 선적 서류에는 20상자인데 세 상자가 부족해요.

B: 손실에 대해서 어떻게 보상해 드릴까요?

A: 다음번에 송장을 작성할 때 360달러를 줄여 작성하시면 어떻겠습니까?

C. Important Points

1. • how soon: 얼마나 빨리
   • direct shipment: 직항 선적
   • a containerized vessel: 컨테이너선

2. • production delays: 생산지연
   • shipping date: 선적일
   • make an agreement with: -와 계약을 맺다
   • on time: 정시에
   • be forced to: -하지 않을 수 없다
   • cancel the contract: 계약을 취소하다

3. • There are very few direct sailings.: 직항선이 거의 없다시피 합니다.
   • They don't sail directly very often.: 직항선이 자주 없습니다.
   • Direct sailings are very few in number.
   직항선의 수가 매우 제한되어 있습니다.

4. • Did you book space on any vessel yet? 선복을 수배해 놓았습니까?
   • 선복(船腹): 배의 중간 허리, 곧 짐을 실을 수 있는 부분
   (=vessel space, space on a vessel)
   • Did you arrange space on any vessel yet? 선복은 확보해 놓았습니까?

5. • be short of: -이 부족하다
   • compensate A for B: A에게 B를 보상하다
   • make out: 작성하다
   • invoice: 송장(送狀)

D. Filling in the Blanks

1. A: How long do you think the shipment will take?

   B: ________________________, about three months or so.

   A: Really? ______________________?

   B: There are very few direct sailings.

   A: That is a problem then, isn't it?

   B: Yeah, but they say ______________________________ starting in two months time.

2. A: ____________________ our order No. 357 of 300 men's jumpers?

   B: This week.

   A: Okay, did you book space ____________________?

   B: Yes, on Amland Line "American Voyager" departing Busan, November 11th.

   A: ____________________ or via Yokohama?

   B: Direct. It arrives in Seattle on November 30th.

3. A: We found that ____________________________ by three boxes.

   B: Really? We are very sorry ________________. I'll just check. (after a while) You are right.

   A: Three boxes against the document, which specifies twenty.

   B: ________________________ for loss?

   A: Why don't you make out the invoice with a reduction of $360 next time?

E. Dictation

1. ______________________________

2. ______________________________

3. ______________________________

4. ______________________________

5. ______________________________

6. ______________________________

7. ______________________________

8. ______________________________

9. ______________________________

10. ______________________________

11. ______________________________

12. ______________________________

13. ______________________________

14. ______________________________

15. ______________________________

E. Dictation 2

1. ____

2. ____

3. ____

4. ____

5. ____

6. ____

7. ____

8. ____

9. ____

10. ____

11. ____

12. ____

13. ____

14. ____

15. ____

PART 2

4. 클레임과 손해배상

4-1 클레임 제기

A. Dialogue

- Listen to the teacher.
- Repeat after the teacher.
- Practice by yourself.
- Memorize the dialogue.

1. A: We have a problem with your products.
   B: What's wrong with them?
   A: Some are heavily damaged due to loose packing.
   This is clearly your error.
   B: We'll do our best to straighten things up.
   A: I think you are forced to answer for any broken products.

2. A: Mr. Smith, I assure you that we followed the specification to the letter.
   B: Then why did it turn out like that?
   A: I'm not sure. I checked everything very carefully every step of the way.
   B: Anyway it's clear that something went wrong somewhere.
   A: Mr. Smith, we put in a lot of time and effort on this product.
   B: I'm sure you did it. But it's the results that count.

B. Practice

- Read through the dialogue in Korean.
- Repeat the dialogue in English.

1. A: 귀사 제품에 문제가 있습니다.
   B: 뭐가 잘못 되었습니까?
   A: 느슨한 포장 때문에 일부가 크게 파손되었습니다.
   이것은 분명히 귀측의 실수입니다.
   B: 잘못된 것을 해결하기 위해 최선을 다하겠습니다.
   A: 파손된 상품에 대해서는 책임을 지셔야 겠습니다.

2. A: 스미스씨, 확실히 말씀드리지만 저희는 작업명세서를 정확히 따랐습니다.
   B: 그렇다면 왜 그런 결과가 나왔지요?
   A: 저도 확실히 모르겠습니다. 단계마다 세심한 주의를 기울여 모든 걸 확인했습니다.
   B: 하여튼, 어딘가에서 뭔가 잘못된 것이 분명합니다.
   A: 스미스씨, 저희는 이 제품에 많은 시간과 노력을 쏟았습니다.
   B: 그렇게 하셨겠지요. 하지만 중요한 것은 결과입니다.

3. A: (on the phone) The order placed on September 7 hasn't arrived yet.
B: Hold on please. I'll call the warehouse and check up on it.
A: Thanks.
B: We are sorry for the late delivery. They sent it three days ago.
A: We are out of stock now.
B: You'll get your goods today or tomorrow.

4. A: Ms. Jenkins, what do you think of our new model?
B: It's good except for one thing.
A: Really? what's that?
B: The little handle on the adjustor keeps coming off.
A: Oh gee! Sorry to hear that. I'll see what can be done to solve it.
B: Please do it. We've already had several complaints about that.

5. A: Mr. Park, Can I ask you a favor?
B: I'll do my best, whatever it is.
A: The product itself is fine. It's the screw caps that are causing problems.
B: What's the matter?
A: Half the time they don't come off.
B: I see. Please don't be afraid. I'll attend to that for you right away and make an effort to solve the matter immediately.

3. A: (전화로) 9월 7일에 주문한 것이 아직 도착하지 않았어요.
B: 끊지 말고 기다리세요. 창고에 전화를 걸어 확인하겠습니다.
A: 고맙습니다.
B: 납품이 늦어서 죄송합니다. 3일전에 보냈습니다.
A: 재고가 다 떨어졌어요.
B: 오늘이나 내일 상품을 받으실 겁니다.

4. A: 젠킨스씨, 저희 새 모델을 어떻게 생각하십니까?
B: 한 가지를 제외하곤 좋습니다.
A: 정말입니까? 그게 뭐지요?
B: 소정장치의 소형 손잡이가 자꾸 빠진답니다.
A: 아이고 저런! 그런 말씀 들으니 죄송하군요. 제가 어떤 해결책이 있나 알아 보겠습니다.
B: 예, 그렇게 해주십시오. 그 것에 대해 이미 몇 건의 불평을 받았어요.

5. A: 박 선생님, 부탁드릴 게 한 가지 있는데요.
B: 어떤 부탁이든 최선을 다해 도와 드려야죠.
A: 제품 자체는 좋습니다. 문제를 일으키는 건 나사뚜껑입니다.
B: 뭐가 문제지요?
A: 열리지 않는 경우가 절반입니다.
B: 알겠습니다. 걱정마세요. 제가 즉시 신경을 써서 문제가 곧 해결되도록 노력해 보겠습니다.

C. Important Points

1.
- loose packing: 느슨한 포장
- straighten up: 해결하다, 청산하다, 정리하다
- broken product: 파손된 제품
- answer for: 책임을 지다, 보증하다
- be forced to: -하지 않을 수 없다

2.
- specification: (작업) 명세서
- to the letter: 문자 그대로, 엄밀히
- turn out: (결과) -이 되다, 결국 -임이 드러나다
- It's the results that count.: 중요한 것은 결과입니다.
- count: 가치가 있다, 중요하다
- It's the end product that counts. 중요한 것은 최종결과입니다.
- In business, it's not ethics that count, but who wins the contract.
  사업에서는 윤리가 중요한 것이 아니라 누가 계약을 따내느냐가 중요하다.

3.
- hold on: (전화 등을) 끊지 않고 기다리다
- warehouse: 창고, 저장소
- check up: 조사하다, 확인하다
- out of stock: 재고가 떨어진, 매진된, 품절된
- We are out of stock now.: 재고가 다 떨어졌어요.

4. • I'll see what can be done to solve it.
제가 어떤 해결책이 있나 알아보겠습니다.
• I'll see if it can be fixed [taken care of].
수리가 될 수 있는지 제가 알아보겠습니다.
• I'll see if I can do something about it.
그 문제에 대하여 어떤 해결책이 있는지를 제가 알아보지요.
• Let me look into it and see what can be done.
제가 그 문제를 조사해 보고 어떤 조치를 취할 수 있는지 알아보겠습니다.
• come off: (단추 등이) 떨어지다, 빠지다, 벗겨지다

5. • I'll attend to that for you right away and make an effort to solve the matter immediately.
제가 즉시 신경을 써서 문제가 곧 해결되도록 노력해 보겠습니다.
• attend to: 유의하다, 주의하다
• I'll take care of that matter. 제가 그 문제를 처리하겠습니다.
• I'll see about that. 제가 그것에 대하여 신경을 쓰겠습니다.
• I'll have them do something about that.
그 문제에 대하여 그들로 하여금 어떤 조치를 취하도록 하겠습니다.
• I'll look into that problem. 제가 그 문제를 알아보겠습니다.

D. Filling in the Blanks

1. A: (on the phone) The order placed on September 7 hasn't arrived yet.
   B: Hold on please. I'll call the warehouse and ________________.
   A: Thanks.
   B: We are sorry ____________________. They sent it three days ago.
   A: We are ________________ now.
   B: You'll get your goods today or tomorrow.

2. A: Ms. Jenkins, what do you think of our new model?
   B: It's good ______________________.
   A: Really? what's that?
   B: The little handle on the adjustor ________________.
   A: Oh gee! Sorry to hear that. I'll see ________________ to solve it.
   B: Please do it. We've already had several complaints about that.

3. A: Mr. Park, Can I ask you a favor?
   B: I'll do my best, __________________.
   A: The product itself is fine. It's the screw caps that are causing problems.
   B: What's the matter?
   A: Half the time ____________________.
   B: I see. Please ____________. I'll attend to that for you right away and make an effort to solve the matter immediately.

E. Dictation

1. ____________________

2. ____________________

3. ____________________

4. ____________________

5. ____________________

6. ____________________

7. ____________________

8. ____________________

9. ____________________

10. ____________________

11. ____________________

12. ____________________

13. ____________________

14. ____________________

15. ____________________

4-2 손해배상

A. Dialogue

- Listen to the teacher.
- Repeat after the teacher.
- Practice by yourself.
- Memorize the dialogue.

1. A: We offer 30% reduction on the total shipment.
   B: However the 30% was not entirely worthless.
   A: I understand. But as a matter of fact, our customer didn't accept about 30% of shipment.
   B: 30% is almost out of the question, why don't we meet each other halfway?
   A: Okay, then let's go to 15%.

2. A: The ship-back clause says if the goods are found to be out of tolerance, we are able to ship them back to America.
   B: Right.
   A: Then you have to pay the freight, of course.
   B: If they are really out of tolerance. Can we have rejected goods returned by freight collect?

B. Practice

- Read through the dialogue in Korean.
- Repeat the dialogue in English.

1. A: 전체 선적분의 30% 가격 할인을 제안합니다.
   B: 그렇지만 30%가 완전히 쓸모 없는 것은 아니었습니다.
   A: 압니다. 하지만 사실 우리 고객이 선적분의 약 30%를 인수 거부했습니다.
   B: 30%는 거의 불가능합니다. 서로 타협하는 것이 어떻습니까?
   A: 좋습니다, 그러면 15%로 하죠.

2. A: 반송 조항에는 상품이 품질 불량이면 미국으로 되돌려 보낼 수 있는 것으로 되어 있습니다.
   B: 그렇습니다.
   A: 그런 경우에는 물론 운임은 귀사가 지불하셔야만 합니다.
   B: 정말로 품질 불량이면 그렇게 해야죠. 반품은 운임 후불로 돌려보내 주시겠습니까?

3. A: Look, Ms. Lee, we've just got to settle this claim somehow.

B: I understand your position, Mr. Green. But, unfortunately we just can't assume full responsibility for it this time.

A: Then that'd leave me no choice but to give it to an international claim settlement company.

B: Oh, I don't think you should go that far. I'm sure we can work something out between ourselves.

A: Well, then, what is your offer?

B: How about settling for half?

4. A: What's wrong with our goods?

B: We've had complaints from our customers.

A: Could you explain the problems in detail?

B: Your last shipment was short by 20 units.

A: Really? I'm very sorrry about that. I'll send the missing units to you shortly.

5. A: What are the contents of the claim clauses?

B: Firstly, we have to define the term of the notice of claim.

A: How many days do you have in mind?

B: The notice of claim must be submitted within 10 days after the arrival of goods at destination.

3. A: 저, 이 선생님, 어떻게든 이 손해배상(청구)는 해결해 주셔야 합니다.
B: 그린씨 입장은 이해합니다. 그러나 이번만큼은 그것에 대해 저희가 책임을 다 질 수는 없습니다.
A: 그러면 국제손해배상중재회사에 넘기는 수밖에는 다른 도리가 없겠군요.
B: 그렇게까지 하시지 않아도 되잖아요. 분명히 우리끼리 해결해 낼 수 있을 겁니다.
A: 저, 그러면 해결방안이 뭐죠?
B: 절반 정도의 금액으로 마무리 지으면 어떨까요?

4. A: 우리 상품의 문제가 뭐죠?
B: 고객들로부터 불만이 있었습니다.
A: 문제를 상세히 설명해 주시겠어요?
B: 지난 번 선적분에 20개가 부족했습니다.
A: 정말입니까? 정말 죄송합니다. 곧 부족분을 보내드리겠습니다.

5. A: 손해 배상 조항의 내용이 뭐죠?
B: 첫째로 손해배상 청구의 통지기간을 정해야만 합니다.
A: 며칠 정도를 마음에 두고 계십니까?
B: 손해배상 청구의 통지는 화물이 목적항에 도착 후 10일 이내에 해야만 합니다.

C. Important Points

1.
- reduction: 할인, 인하, 축소
- meet a person halfway: 타협하다, 서로 다가서다

2.
- the ship-back clause: 반송조항
- out of tolerance: 품질 불량
- ship something back: 반송하다
- pay the freight: 운임을 지불하다
- rejected goods: 반품
- freight collect: 운임 후불

3.
- We just can't assume full responsibility for it this time.
  이번만큼은 그것에 대해 우리가 모든 책임을 다 질 수 없습니다.
- assume: (책임, 의무 등을) 떠맡다
- You can't expect us to be entirely responsible for it.
  우리가 모든 책임을 질 것을 기대해서는 안 됩니다.
- You can't put all the blame on us.
  모든 책임을 우리에게 지울 수는 없습니다.
- You have to share some of the blame.
  귀사 측에서도 책임의 일부를 져야 합니다.
- You made some mistakes, too. 귀사의 잘못도 있는 것입니다.

4.
- missing units: 분실분
- shortly: 곧, 이내

5.
- claim clause: 손해배상 청구조항
- the term of the notice of claim: 손해배상 청구 통지기간
- destination: 목적지, 행선지, 도착지

D. Filling in the Blanks

1. A: Look, Ms. Lee, we've just got to settle this claim somehow.
   B: I understand ____________, Mr. Green. But, unfortunately we just can't assume ________________________ this time.
   A: Then that'd leave me no choice but to give it to an international claim settlement company.
   B: Oh, I don't think ______________________. I'm sure we can work something out between ourselves.
   A: Well, then, what is your offer?
   B: How about settling for half?

2. A: What's wrong with our goods?
   B: We've had ______________________________.
   A: Could you explain __________________________?
   B: __________________________________ by 20 units.
   A: Really? I'm very sorry about that. I'll send the missing units to you shortly.

3. A: What are _________________________________?
   B: Firstly, we have to define the term of the notice of claim.
   A: How many days __________________________?
   B: The notice of claim must be submitted ______________ after the arrival of goods at destination.

E. Dictation

1. ______________________________

2. ______________________________

3. ______________________________

4. ______________________________

5. ______________________________

6. ______________________________

7. ______________________________

8. ______________________________

9. ______________________________

10. ______________________________

11. ______________________________

12. ______________________________

13. ______________________________

14. ______________________________

15. ______________________________

E. Dictation 2

1. ______________________________

2. ______________________________

3. ______________________________

4. ______________________________

5. ______________________________

6. ______________________________

7. ______________________________

8. ______________________________

9. ______________________________

10. ______________________________

11. ______________________________

12. ______________________________

13. ______________________________

14. ______________________________

15. ______________________________

PART 2

5. 해외 출장

5-1 해외 출장 일반회화

A. Dialogue

- Listen to the teacher.
- Repeat after the teacher.
- Practice by yourself.
- Memorize the dialogue.

1. A: Excuse me, can you cash this traveller's check for me?
B: Yes, sir, do you have any ID?
A: ID? I'm sorry. I don't understand. What do you mean by ID?
B: Identification. Driver's license, for example.
A: I'm sorry. I don't have a driver's license. How about my passport?
B: That'll do, sir.

2. A: Please have a seat here, sir.
B: Thanks. I'd like to have my hair cut in the back and on the sides, but not on the top.
A: Okay, sir. How would you like your hair parted?
B: Part my hair on the right side, please.
A: Okay, would you care for a shampoo later, sir?
B: No, just a haircut will be fine, thanks.

Business English Conversation

B. Practice

- Read through the dialogue in Korean.
- Repeat the dialogue in English.

1. A: 실례합니다. 이 여행자수표를 현금으로 좀 바꿔주시겠습니까?
   B: 예, ID가지고 계세요?
   A: ID요? 미안하지만 무슨 말씀인지 모르겠는데요. ID가 뭐지요?
   B: 신분증이요. 가령 운전면허증 같은 것 말입니다.
   A: 죄송합니다. 운전면허증이 없는데요. 여권은 안 될까요?
   B: 그것이면 됩니다.

2. A: 여기로 앉으십시오. 손님.
   B: 감사합니다. 뒷머리와 옆머리를 잘라주세요. 위는 자르지 말고요.
   A: 예, 알겠습니다. 가르마는 어느 쪽으로 탈까요?
   B: 오른쪽으로 타 주십시오.
   A: 예. 나중에 샴푸를 하시겠습니까?
   B: 아니, 괜찮습니다. 그냥 머리만 잘라주십시오.

3. A: Oh, I'm sorry, I left my key in the room.
B: That's all right. We can solve the problem.
The bellboy will let you in.
A: Thank you. By the way, are there any messages for me?
B: Just a minute. Can you give me your room number, sir?

4. A: Would you fill her up with unleaded, please?
B: Certainly, sir. How about the oil? Would you like to check it?
A: Yes, please. And check the brake and transmission fluid, too.
B: Sure, sir. Your left rear tire looks a little low.
A: Oh, really? Put some air in it, please.
How much does it cost in all?
B: That will be $47.20.

5. A: Hi, please be seated here. What's the problem?
B: I have a severe migraine.
A: Have you had enough sleep in the past few days?
B: No, I was quite busy to do the business here.
A: I see. It doesn't look like anything serious to me.
But you have to have enough rest.
B: That's a relief. How long do I have to rest?
A: Just a full day.
B: Then can I continue the business and trip?
A: Sure, I will write out a prescription for you.

3. A: 미안합니다만 객실에다 열쇠를 두고 나왔어요.
B: 괜찮습니다. 문제를 해결할 수 있습니다.
벨보이가 문을 열어 드릴 겁니다.
A: 고맙습니다. 그런데 내게 연락온 것은 없습니까?
B: 잠깐만요. 방번호를 알려 주시겠습니까?

4. A: 무연휘발유로 가득 채워 주시겠어요?
B: 그러겠습니다, 손님. 엔진 오일은 어떻게 하시겠습니까?
확인해 보시겠습니까?
A: 네, 그러죠. 브레이크와 트랜스미션 용액도 확인해 주세요.
B: 알겠습니다. 왼쪽 뒷타이어에 바람이 좀 적은 것 같습니다.
A: 정말입니까? 공기를 좀 넣어 주세요. 모두 얼마죠?
B: 47달러 20센트입니다.

5. A: 안녕하세요, 여기 앉으세요. 어디가 아프세요?
B: 편두통이 심해요.
A: 지난 며칠동안 충분히 수면을 취했습니까?
B: 아니오. 이곳에서 업무를 보느라고 매우 바빴습니다.
A: 알겠습니다. 제가 보기엔 대단한 것 같지는 않습니다.
하지만 휴식을 충분히 취하셔야만 합니다.
B: 안심입니다. 휴식을 얼마나 취해야 할까요?
A: 하루 푹 쉬면 됩니다.
B: 그리고 나서는 업무와 (업무)여행을 계속할 수 있을까요?
A: 물론이죠. 처방전을 써 드리겠습니다.

C. Important Points

1. • Excuse me, Can you cash this traveller's check for me?
   죄송합니다만 이 여행자수표를 현금으로 좀 바꿔주실 수 있습니까?
   • cash: 현금, 맞돈. (어음 따위를) 현찰로 바꾸다
   • Can I cash this traveller's check here?
   여행자수표를 여기서 현금으로 바꿀 수 있습니까?
   • Where can I get this check cashed?
   이 수표를 어디 가면 현금으로 바꿀 수 있습니까?
   • Can I pay by traveller's check?: 여행자수표로 지급해도 됩니까?
   • Can I use this credit card here?
   여기서 이 신용카드의 사용이 가능합니까?
   • Please endorse this check.: 이 수표에 이서를 해주십시오.
   • Can I have another person cash this traveller's check for me?
   저 대신 다른 사람이 이 수표를 현금으로 바꿀 수 있습니까?

2. 〈이발과 관련된 표현〉
   • Please part my hair on the right side. 가르마는 오른쪽으로 타 주십시오.
   • Please part my hair in the middle. 가르마는 중간 가르마를 타 주십시오.
   • Cut my hair in the same style as it is, please.
   머리를 현재의 스타일로 깎아 주세요.
   • I'm in a hurry. Can you do it in an hour?
   시간이 없는데 1시간 이내에 깎을 수 있습니까?
   • Just a trim only, please.
   (머리모양은 바꾸지 말고) 조금만 쳐 주세요.
   • The barber gave me a poor trim.
   그 이발사는 내 머리를 엉성하게 깎아 주었다.
   • Would you care for a shave? 면도를 하시겠습니까?

- Don't take too much off the sides. 옆 부분을 너무 많이 깎지 마세요.
- How much do you charge for a haircut only?
  머리만 깎는 데 요금이 얼마입니까?
- I'd like to have my hair dried.: 머리를 좀 말려 주십시오.

3.
- bellboy: (호텔, 클럽의) 사환 (=bellhop)
- by the way: 도중에, 말이 난 김에, 그런데
- Are there any messages for me?: 내게 연락 온 것 없습니까?
- Can you give me your room number, sir?
  방번호를 알려 주시겠습니까?

4.
- Would you fill her up with unleaded, please?
  무연휘발유로 가득 채워 주시겠어요?
- fill up: (가득) 채우다
- 자동차를 여성 she (her)로 표현하는 경우도 있다.

5.
- migraine: 편두통
- It doesn't look like anything serious to me.
  제가 보기엔 대단한 것 같지는 않습니다.
- That's a relief.: 안심입니다.
- I will write out a prescription for you.
  처방전을 써 드리겠습니다.
- prescription: 처방전

D. Filling in the Blanks

1. A: Oh, I'm sorry, I left my key in the room.
   B: That's all right. ____________________. The bellboy will let you in.
   A: Thank you. By the way, ____________________ for me?
   B: Just a minute. Can you give me ____________________, sir?

2. A: Would you fill her up with unleaded, please?
   B: Certainly, sir. How about the oil? ____________________?
   A: Yes, please. And check the brake and transmission fluid, too.
   B: Sure, sir. Your left rear tire ____________________.
   A: Oh, really? ____________________, please. How much does it cost in all?
   B: That will be $47.20.

3. A: Hi, please be seated here. What's the problem?
   B: I have ____________________.
   A: Have you had enough sleep in the past few days?
   B: No, I was quite busy ____________________ here.
   A: I see. It doesn't look like anything serious to me. But you have to have enough rest.
   B: ____________________. How long do I have to rest?
   A: Just a full day.
   B: Then can I continue the business and trip?
   A: Sure, I will write out a prescription for you.

E. Dictation

1. ______

2. ______

3. ______

4. ______

5. ______

6. ______

7. ______

8. ______

9. ______

10. ______

11. ______

12. ______

13. ______

14. ______

15. ______

5-2 업무관련 상담 및 대화

A. Dialogue

- Listen to the teacher.
- Repeat after the teacher.
- Practice by yourself.
- Memorize the dialogue.

1. 1-a

A: I would like to tell you, Young-Ho, I am not in favor of this idea of yours. The last time we tried to export we wasted lots of time and money.

B: Well, I wasn't here then. But breaking into export is always difficult.

A: Certainly, one problem is we're struggling to maintain our markets right here in the states.

B: But, Peter, the Indonesian market looks promising. In this instance, I think the odds are in our favor.

B. Practice

- Read through the dialogue in Korean.
- Repeat the dialogue in English.

1. 1-a

A: 영호씨, 당신에게 말하고 싶은 것이 있어요. 나는 당신의 의견에 찬성하지 않습니다. 우리가 지난번에 수출하려고 했을 때 우리는 많은 시간과 돈을 낭비했어요.

B: 음, 전 그 때 여기에 없었어요. 하지만 수출을 새롭게 여는 것은 항상 어렵죠.

A: 그렇습니다. 문제는 우리가 바로 여기 미국에서 우리의 시장을 유지하려고 고투하고 있는 것이에요.

B: 하지만 피터씨 인도네시아 시장은 유망해 보여요. 이 경우에 승산은 우리에게 있어요.

1-b

A: Well, if so please tell me your case.

B: To begin with, the Ministry of Foreign Affairs and Trade is really enthusiastic about it and they've promised their support.

A: Then what are they going to do?

B: They've already sent an e-mail and a fax to the commercial attache in Indonesia, so we wouldn't have any problems getting the necessary licenses and permits. In addition the Ministry promised to process our documents without delay. We could negotiate an offer immediately!

A: Amazing! Our government is certainly doing everything they can these days to support companies to export.

B: Statistics show that the market for cell phones is developing rapidly in Indonesia, and that their credit status is good.

1-c

A: It seems optimistic. By the way, when are you going to go to Indonesia?

B: The special report from the attache should be here by next Friday. After reading it, I could be ready to leave.

A: Okay. Good luck with your trip.

1-b

A: 음, 그렇다면 당신의 경우를 얘기해 주세요.

B: 우선 외교통상부가 정말로 그것에 대해 열심이고 지원해 주기로 약속했어요.

A: 그렇다면 그 사람들은 무엇을 할 거죠?

B: 그들은 이미 전자 우편과 팩스를 인도네시아에 있는 상무관에게 보냈어요. 그래서 우린 필요한 인가와 허가를 얻는데 아무 문제가 없을 겁니다. 게다가 외교통상부는 우리의 서류를 지체 없이 처리해 주기로 약속했어요. 우리는 즉시 청약을 협상할 수 있습니다!

A: 놀랍군요! 우리 정부는 요즈음 수출을 하려는 회사를 지원해 주기 위해 확실히 그들이 할 수 있는 모든 것을 하고 있어요.

B: 인도네시아에서 휴대폰 시장이 빠르게 커가고 있다는 것을 통계가 보여줍니다. 그리고 그들의 신용상태가 좋다는 것도요.

1-c

A: 낙관적인 것 같군요. 그런데 언제 인도네시아로 가실 겁니까?

B: 상무관으로부터의 특별 보고서가 다음주 금요일까지는 이곳에 도착할 겁니다. 그걸 읽고 떠날 준비를 할 수 있을 것 같습니다.

A: 그렇군요. 여행 잘 다녀오세요.

2. 2-a

A: Excuse me, are you Ms. Blake from Canada?

B: Yes, I am. I guess you are Mr. Yong-Joon Kim?

A: Yes. How do you do?

B: Nice to meet you.

A: How was your trip? You must have jet lag.

B: Yes, I do. Otherwise everything is fine. And I like the Korean hospitality.

A: Oh, thank you. Shall we go to the company?

B: Alright.

2-b

A: Here we are.

B: Oh, it's very close. Can I ask when your company was established?

A: We started our business in 1972. We have enjoyed a good reputation for quality control and after-sale service from the beginning.

B: Can I ask how many outlets deal your products?

A: Of course, we have more than 500 outlets nationwide and 35 of those are in Asian countries.

B: I see. Are there any branch offices in Japan or China?

A: Yes, we have two branch offices in Japan. One in Osaka and the other in Tokyo.

B: Very good. Do you have any plans to open branches in Canada?

A: Not at the moment. But I overheard that our CEO is planning something in Canada. Shall we go on a factory tour?

B: Okay. But first let me wash my hands.

A: Sure, please go down the hall and turn right.

2. 2-a

A: 실례합니다만, 캐나다에서 오신 블레이크양이신지요?

B: 네, 그런데요. 혹시 김용준씨 되시나요?

A: 네, 그렇습니다. 처음 뵙겠습니다.

B: 만나 뵙게 되어 반갑습니다.

A: 여행 어떠셨어요? 시차에서 오는 피로 때문에 힘드시죠?

B: 네, 그래요. 여행 피로감을 제외하곤 다 좋습니다. 특히 한국분들이 참 친절하시네요.

A: 아 그러세요, 감사합니다. 회사로 가실까요?

B: 좋습니다.

2-b

A: 다 왔습니다.

B: 아 정말 가깝군요. 회사의 창립연도를 여쭤봐도 될까요?

A: 1972년에 창립했지요. 그 후 계속 '품질 관리'와 '애프터서비스' 분야에 있어 탁월하다는 소리를 꾸준히 듣고 있습니다.

B: 귀사의 상품을 취급하는 대리점이 몇 곳 있는지 여쭤 봐도 될까요?

A: 그럼요. 국내엔 500군데 이상의 대리점이 있고 아시아 국가들엔 35군데의 대리점이 있어요.

B: 알겠습니다. 일본이나 중국에 지사가 있나요?

A: 네, 일본에 두 곳의 지사가 있죠. 하나는 '오사카'에 있고 다른 하나는 '토쿄'에 있습니다.

B: 굉장하군요. 캐나다에 지사를 설립하실 의향은 없으신가요?

A: 현재로선 없습니다. 그런데 저희 회사의 회장님께서 캐나다에 뭔가를 계획하고 있으시다고 들었습니다. 저희 공장을 한번 보시겠습니까?

B: 알겠습니다. 우선 화장실 좀 다녀오겠습니다.

A: 네, 복도를 따라 가시다가 오른쪽으로 돌아가세요.

2-c

〈a few minutes later〉

A: This is our factory. What do you think of this?

B: It's great. You have nice facilities and an efficient production line. it's really impressive. By the way how big is the factory?

A: Our factory has an area of 8000 square meters and three hundred forty five employees are currently working here. We are going to build a second plant near the bay area.

B: Oh, Amazing. Can I see the goods from the company? I am especially interested in Digital cameras and DVD players.

A: Okay, shall we go back to the conference room?

2-d

A: These are the products we are making and you can look at the catalog for more detailed information.

B: Excellent, what are the terms of payment?

A: For foreign markets, twenty percent of the total is due when the order is received, and the rest of the total payment is due when the goods are delivered to the company. If you pay on a cash basis, you can take advantage of a 10 percent discount.

2-c

〈잠시 후〉

A: 여기가 저희 공장입니다. 어떠세요?

B: 훌륭하군요. 시설도 훌륭하고 생산라인도 아주 효율적으로 배치되어 있습니다. 정말 인상적입니다. 그런데 공장은 얼마나 크지요?

A: 저희 공장의 면적은 8000 제곱 미터이고 현재 345명의 직원이 근무하고 있습니다. 가까운 시일 내에 항만 가까이에 제2 공장을 건설할 예정입니다.

B: 아 놀랍군요. 생산 상품을 좀 볼 수 있을까요? 저는 디지털 카메라와 DVD 재생기에 특히 관심이 있습니다.

A: 좋습니다. 회의실로 돌아가서 이야기 하실까요?

2-d

A: 이 제품들이 저희 회사가 생산하는 품목이죠. 그리고 카타로그를 보시면 더 자세한 정보를 얻으실 수 있지요.

B: 훌륭하군요. 지불 조건이 어떻게 되나요?

A: 외국 시장에는 물품 주문을 받을 때 총 금액의 20 퍼센트를 선불로 지불해야 하며 나머지는 물품이 회사로 배달될 때 지불되야 합니다. 현찰 구매시는 10 퍼센트의 할인 혜택이 주어집니다.

C. Important Points

1. 1-a

- Breaking into export is always difficult.
  수출을 새롭게 여는 것은 항상 어렵죠.
- The odds are in our favor.
  승산은 우리에게 있어요.

1-b

- The Ministry of Foreign Affairs and Trade: 외교통상부
- commercial attache: 상무관
- Their credit status is good.: 그들의 신용상태는 좋습니다.

1-c

- optimistic: 낙관적인
- The special report from the attache should be here by next Friday.
  상무관으로부터의 특별 보고서가 다음주 금요일까지는 이곳에 도착할 겁니다.
- Good luck with your trip.: 여행 잘 다녀오세요.

2. 2-a

- jet lag: 비행기 여행을 장시간 한 후 시차가 많이 나는 지역에서 활동할 때 나타나는 피로현상
- hospitality: 환대, 친절히 접대함

2-b

- Can I ask when your company was established?
  회사의 창립연도를 여쭤봐도 될까요?
- quality control: 품질관리
- after-sale service: 애프터서비스
- Can I ask how many outlets deal your products?
  귀사의 상품을 취급하는 대리점이 몇 곳 있는지 여쭤 봐도 될까요?
- CEO: Chief Executive Officer 의 준말, '최고 경영자', '회장'
- Let me wash my hands.: 화장실 좀 다녀오겠습니다.
- wash hands: '화장실엘 다녀오겠다'는 의미의 표현
- Where can I wash my hands?: 화장실이 어디죠?
- down the hall: '복도를 따라가다'

2-c

- You have nice facilities and an efficient production line.
  시설도 훌륭하고 생산라인도 아주 효율적으로 배치되어 있습니다.
- We are going to build a second plant near the bay area.
  가까운 시일 내에 항만 가까이에 제2 공장을 건설할 예정입니다.
- I am especially interested in Digital cameras and DVD players.
  저는 디지털 카메라와 DVD 재생기에 특히 관심이 있습니다.

2-d

- terms of payment: 지불조건
- due: 지불 기일이 된, 당연히 치러야 할
- on a cash basis: 현금으로

D. Filling in the Blanks

1. A: I would like to tell you, Young-Ho, ____________________ this idea of yours. The last time we tried to export we wasted lots of time and money.

   B: Well, ____________________. But breaking into export is always difficult.

   A: Certainly, one problem is we're struggling ________________________ right here in the states.

   B: But, Peter, the Indonesian market looks promising. In this instance, I think the odds are in our favor.

2. A: Excuse me, ______________________________?

   B: Yes, I am. I guess you are Mr. Yong-Joon Kim?

   A: Yes. How do you do?

   B: Nice to meet you.

   A: How was your trip? ______________________________.

   B: Yes, I do. ____________________________. And I like the Korean hospitality.

   A: Oh, thank you. Shall we go to the company?

   B: Alright.

3. A: This is our factory. What do you think of this?

B: It's great. You have nice facilities and an efficient production line. it's really impressive. By the way ________________________?

A: Our factory has an area of 8000 square meters and three hundred forty five employees are ____________________. We are going to build a second plant near the bay area.

B: Oh, Amazing. Can I see ________________________? I am especially interested in Digital cameras and DVD players.

A: Okay, shall we go back to the conference room?

E. Dictation

1. ______

2. ______

3. ______

4. ______

5. ______

6. ______

7. ______

8. ______

9. ______

10. ______

11. ______

12. ______

13. ______

14. ______

15. ______

부록

비즈니스 영어회화에서 나온
중요한 표현 목록

A

a feather in one's cap[hat] 훌륭한 업적; 자랑[영광]이 되는 것
a sort of 일종의, ~와 같은 것
adaptability 적응성, 순응성, 융통성
advising bank 통지은행
after-sale(s) service 애프터서비스
agreement 계약(서)
aisle seat 통로측 좌석
allocate 배분하다, …을 배치하다 (=apply, place)
amend 수정하다
amendment 수정
answer for 책임을 지다, 보증하다
apply for the L/C 신용장 개설을 신청하다.
as fit as a fiddle 건강하여, 원기 왕성하여
assume (책임, 의무 등을) 떠맡다
attend to 유의하다, 주의하다

B

balance 차액, 차감잔액
balcony seat (극장의) 2층 좌석
be forced to ~하지 않을 수 없다
be short of ~이 부족하다
be sold on 좋다고 믿다, 찬성하다.
be up for (진급 · 재판 · 시험 등의) 대상으로 오르다.
beeper 삐삐
bellboy (호텔, 클럽의) 사환 (=bellhop)
bring down 물가를 떨어뜨리다, 가격을 내리다
broken product 파손된 제품
buck (미 구어) 남자, 멋쟁이
Business class 비즈니스 클래스 좌석
by the way 도중에, 말이 난 김에, 그런데

C

call for ~을 요구하다, ~을 필요로 하다
cancel the contract 계약을 취소하다
cannon 대포
care to ~ ~하고 싶어하다 = would you care to ~?
cash 현금, 맞돈; (어음 따위를) 현찰로 바꾸다
CEO Chief Executive Officer 의 준말, '최고 경영자', '회장'
change 거스름돈
check up 조사하다, 확인하다
chowder 생선 혹은 조개에 절인 돼지고기, 양파 등을 섞어 끓인 것.
CIF 운임, 보험료 포함가격 (Cost, insurance and freight)
circulation 혈액 순환
claim clause 손해배상 청구조항
claustrophobic 밀실 공포증의, 밀실 공포증 환자
collect call = reverse charge call 수신자 부담 전화
come down 값을 내리다
come off (단추 등이) 떨어지다, 빠지다, 벗겨지다
commercial attache 상무관
compensate A for B A에게 B를 보상하다
containerized vessel 컨테이너선
contract 계약, 계약서
count 가치가 있다, 중요하다
current 흐름, 전류, 경향

D

delivery 인도
dessert 후식
destination 목적지, 행선지, 도착지
direct shipment 직항 선적
display window 진열장
down the hall '복도를 따라가다'
drop into ~에 잠시 들르다 (=stop by)

drop over 느닷없이 가다(미국의 구어체 표현)
due 지불 기일이 된, 당연히 치러야 할
durable 오래 견디는, 튼튼한
during one's stay in the U.S. as a student 미국 유학 중에
Duty Free shop 면세점

E

early delivery 조기 인도
Economy class 이코노미 클래스 좌석
edge 우세, 우세한 점
exact specifications 정확한 규격

F

fabric 피륙, 직물, 천, 구조, 조직
fill (주문을) 받다, ~을 이행하다, 충족시키다.
fill up (가득) 채우다
FOB 본선 인도 (=Free on Board)
for the time being 당분간, 우선은
fort 성채, 요새, 보루
freight collect 운임 후불
french fries 감자를 채 썰어서 튀긴 것.
fully booked 빈 방이 없다.

G

get down 적어두다 (write, note, record)
get together 모이다, 화합하다.
go ahead and 어서 (구어로 재촉하는 뜻)
grate 비비다, 문지르다, 뭉개다
gun 대포, 포, 총

H

hold on (전화 등을) 끊지 않고 기다리다
hospitality 환대, 친절히 접대함
How about -ing? 혹은 명사 ~하는 게 어때? ~는 어떻습니까?
how soon 얼마나 빨리

I

I'll be happy to~ 기뻐서 ~하다.
ID (=identification) 신분증. 주민등록증, 운전면허증, 학생증 등이 여기에 해당된다.
in regard to ~에 관한, ~에 관해서
in the reign of ~의 왕대에, ~의 치세에
inspection certificate 검사 보고서, 검품 보고서
invoice 송장 (送狀)

J

jet lag 비행기 여행을 장시간 한 후 시차가 많이 나는 지역에서 활동할 때 나타나는 피로현상

L

L/C 신용장 (=Letter of Credit)
leave out 생략하다, 제외하다
like a charm 신통하게, 신기하게
line 선박회사, 선사
loose packing 느슨한 포장

M

M.S. 발동기선 (=Motor Ship)
make an agreement with ~와 계약을 맺다
make it - 목표를 달성 하다, (일을) 잘 해내다

- (약속장소, 시간, 가격 따위를) ~로 하다
- 제 시간에 대다.

make out (문서 등을)작성하다
make up the contract 계약서를 작성하다
meet 맞추다, 만족시키다, 응하다
meet a person halfway 타협하다, 서로 다가서다
migraine 편두통
missing units 분실분
mobile phone 휴대폰 (=cellular phone, cell phone)

O

on a cash basis 현금으로
on a studying abroad 유학으로
on one's mind 마음에 걸리다
on the move 이동 중에
on time 정시에
open 항공기 번호와 탑승시간은 미정으로 해두고 예약을 하는 것.
opening 빈 좌석
opening bank 개설은행
optimistic 낙관적인
orchestra seat 아래층 무대 전면 좌석
order detail 주문 명세서
out of stock 재고가 떨어진, 매진된, 품절된
out of tolerance 품질 불량

P

partial shipment 분할 선적
party 일행
pay phone 공중전화
pay the freight 운임을 지불하다
person to person call 대화자 지명통화
phone booth 공중전화 박스

place an order 주문하다
port of call 방문하는 항구, 기항
prescription 처방전
production delays 생산지연
purchase order sheet 구매 주문서
put someone down 리스트에 ~의 이름을 적다

Q

quality control 품질관리
quote 견적하다, 시가를 말하다

R

recipe 요리법
reduction 할인, 인하, 축소
refer to 참조하다
refund 환불하다
regent 섭정(攝政)
rejected goods 반품
repeat order 재주문
return 반품하다.
rock-bottom price 최저 가격, 최하 가격
route (사람, 여행을 위한) 노선을 정하다, 여행경로[코스]를 정하다

S

ship something back 반송하다
shipment 선적, 선하, 적하위탁화물
shipment 선적, 수송, 발송
shipping date 선적일
shortly 곧, 이내
skillet 프라이팬, 스튜남비
sold out 매진된

space 선복(船腹). 배의 중간 허리, 곧 짐을 실을 수 있는 부분(=vessel space, space on a vessel)
specification (작업) 명세서
spell out 자세히 설명하다
standard practice 표준관행, 표준관례 (=normal way, usual way)
station to station call 번호를 통한 통화
straighten up 해결하다, 청산하다, 정리하다
study abroad at government expenses 국비로 유학하다
study abroad for a number of years 다년간 해외에서 유학하다
suit ~에 적합하다, 어울리다.
suit all tastes 어느 사람에게나 맞다.
suit one down to the ground 안성맞춤이다.
suit yourself 마음대로 하시오, 싫으면 그만두시오.
suite room 침실에 거실, 주방, 욕실 등이 갖춰진 대형 객실을 의미함.
suppose ~라고 가정하다

T

take a look at = look at 보다
take care of 책임지다, 처리하다
terms of payment 지불조건
the Ministry of Foreign Affairs and Trade 외교통상부
the party (전화 받은) 상대방, 당사자
the ship-back clause 반송조항
the term of the notice of claim 손해배상 청구 통지기간
think over 재고하다, 숙고하다
to begin with 우선
to one's advantage ~에게 유리하게[한], ~에게 안성맞춤으로
to the letter 문자 그대로, 엄밀히
try on 입어보다
turn out (결과) ~이 되다, 결국 ~임이 드러나다

V

vacancy 빈 방
vessel 큰 배

W

warehouse 창고, 저장소
warranty (품질 등의) 보증, 보증서
warship 군함, 전함
wash hands '화장실엘 다녀오겠다'는 의미의 표현
wear 입다, 사용에 견디다, 쓸 수 있다, 오래가다
weave (wove-woven) 짜다, 짜맞추다, 뜨다
when it comes (down) to ~에 관해서는
window seat 창측 좌석
wonder ~이 아닐까 생각하다
would [should] have p.p. …했(었)더라면 좋았다, 하고 싶었다

Y

yarn 직물을 짜는 실, 뜨개실

about the Author

박 시 균

전) 청강문화산업대학 비즈니스영어과 교수 / 학과장

전) 인하공업전문대학 교양과 영어담당 교수

현) 군산대학교 인문대학 국어국문학과 교수(외국어로서의 한국어 교육 전공)